APARTMENT BUILDINGS THAT OUTPERFORM

How to Build a Multi-Family Portfolio That Lasts

By Chris Davies

Copyright © Chris Davies, 2016

All Rights Reserved

DEDICATION

This book is dedicated to the memory of my grandfather, William Stanley Davies. I many ways it was his actions that first put me on the path to this book, to success in real estate and to positively impacting the lives of my tenants, owners, family and friends. His wisdom and candour about his failures as well as his successes are deeply missed.

ACKNOWLEDGEMENTS

I hope this book will be a positive part of my legacy. It is already a product of the legacy that came before me, generations of those involved in building, managing and transacting real estate. I'm greatly indebted to a large number of owners, friends and co-workers who have helped me in my career, as well as those who have given their time to this book project.

First, I have to give thanks to God for the extraordinary bit of creation I've been blessed to live in, the people He's set in my life and the unceasing love I see and feel every day. Zander Robertson, my long suffering and massively patient editor, without whom this book would never have seen the light of day. My family, particularly my wife Megan and my boys (Alex, Sam and Luke) who gave me peace and quiet to get this project done. My parents Brent and Leigh, for their love, support and advice, as well as the years of experience working together.

I'm particularly indebted to Don Campbell, one of the most helpful authors I know, as well as Jeff Gunther, Carolyn Davies, Julie Broad, Quentin DeSouza, Pierre Paul Turgeon, Mark Loeffler, AJ Slivinski, Thomas Beyer, Terry Paranych, Russell Westcott, Barry McGuire, Brian Persaud and all the other folks who have given freely of their time, advice and inspiration.

TABLE OF CONTENTS

Introduction: Build Staying Power 1

Chapter 1: The Legacy Strategy 23

Chapter 2: The Niche Strategy 35

Chapter 3: Niche Strategy – Geography 47

Chapter 4: Niche Strategy – Demographics 71

Chapter 5: The Value Chain Strategy – Optimization 89

Chapter 6: Value Chain Strategy – Valuation and Financing . 97

Chapter 7: Value Chain Strategy – Land and Zoning 119

Chapter 8: The Value Chain Strategy – Operations 129

Chapter 9: Value Chain Strategy – Physical Building 147

Chapter 10: The Solidifying Strategy 159

Chapter 11: Wrapping it All Up 169

Appendix: Metrics for your Real Estate Portfolio A-1

INTRODUCTION
Build Staying Power

> "Most people overestimate what they can do in one year and underestimate what they can do in 10 years."
>
> — Bill Gates

Turn Pro

Property management brats have the best real estate stories. I know because I was one. To this day, whenever I meet another property management brat, I find myself laughing at the surreal experiences we share.

I mowed the (scraggly) lawns of run-down apartment buildings in Edmonton's dodgiest neighborhoods while my friends were at summer camp. I changed locks, painted hallways, and learned to assess the safety of balconies from a young age. Who could forget the joys of sweeping parking lots (my first real job) or picking up used needles from the properties we managed?

Something not uncommonly heard in my world: "We need to evict an angry 6'2 alcoholic. Let's send in the 110-pound pimply faced 14-year-old." That was me (the pimply faced one, not the angry alcoholic one).

Then there was the time I discovered the rotting corpse of a young man who committed suicide. You see it all in property management.

Of course there were times I hated it. Even at a young age I could sense that there was something special about this business of real estate. It was more than bricks and mortar. It was more than income and expenses. It was more than the relationships with tenants.

Trying to figure out what made investors successful was like putting together a large and complex puzzle. Different parts didn't make sense until other parts were put together first. There was an attitude amongst the best – an ability to execute and just *get it done* – about the most successful of the investors we dealt with through my family's property management business. I found myself drawn into studying and learning how those great investors ticked.

Over the years, several conclusions have become obvious to me. This book is collected wisdom from all of my years in the real estate industry, starting from the bottom in property management, through my experiences as an investor and a multi-family realtor.

Let's back up for a moment.

My family's primary business was property management. We were (and are) also an investing family.

My grandpa had a significant portfolio, which my dad added to. I was born into a legacy of sorts, but experience with different types of investors taught me to take nothing for granted.

Real estate portfolios can be lost much easier than they can be earned.

Listening to my grandpa and the story of how he went into the great recession of the 1980s with 17 properties and came out with only three, taught a valuable lesson. To build true legacy, you need staying power. To obtain staying power you need strategy. This was the time of the National Energy Policy, a political decision that alienated provinces like Alberta and cities like Ottawa, causing many Albertans to lose their fortunes.

We could blame the elder Trudeau and the Ottawa architects of the NEP. But recessions happen from time-to-time, with or without government help.

As investors, we need to consider this fact with a clear head. Rather than blame real estate failures on the economy or the government, we must learn how to recession-proof our investments. This question has driven much of my thinking on the subject and many of my actions as an investor and real estate agent. It's great to buy and own real estate, but how do you do it properly? How do you avoid my family's 1980s fate?

The answer became clearer to me over the years as I saw investor-after-investor come and go. They arrived in the business full of hopes, dreams, and goals – huge goals. They wanted to buy everything. The common misperception shared by all the flash-in-the-pan investors was that owning more real estate would result in more success, more money, and more income.

They lacked vision. Rather than seeking legacy and thinking in terms of staying power, they thought in terms of riches. Real estate was a means-to-an-end for them.

It's a psychological minefield out there in the real estate industry.

The point of investing in real estate is to create, grow and sustain wealth. Yet, real estate isn't a vehicle that will provide enough cash flow to live a lifestyle – at least not right away.

It can be done, but I don't know many investors that have become full-time investors right away.

In spite of all the evidence against this dream the myth of the investor living off cash flow still survives.

For those who do eventually become full time real estate investors, the journey is usually a minimum of 10 years. There's a school of thought (and I subscribe to this belief) that it takes at least 10,000 hours to become a true expert, to master any field.

Real estate investing is no different.

10 years and/or 10,000 hours can feel like a long time at the beginning, but it's a worthy goal. Getting to full time as a real estate investor is different than other fields because in addition to needing expertise, we also need to

survive recessions, carry debt through slowing economies, and maintain our energy through it all.

We need staying power.

Multi-Family Investing Rule: For every hour spent planning and acting for growth, investors must also spend an hour planning and acting for staying power.

I have seen too many real estate investors come and go, their fortunes ebbing and flowing, their energy levels raising and falling. I've seen investors sink into depression, and it got bad for some of them – real bad.

Others were able to pull out of it.

Here's the trouble: it (usually) only becomes clear that more real estate won't solve an investor's problems until the psychological cost has been tallied. The real estate investor myth is that more will solve your problems.

The truth is, without an effective strategy, more real estate will only cause more problems. Many investors believe random buying equals real estate success. There is misplaced faith in the market's ability to solve problems caused by lack of strategy.

Time, paying attention, managing family assets, and practicing with my own investments have provided me some unique insights. Some investors succeed in the multi-family arena and others don't. This book is about the difference. It's about amateur and pro investment approaches. Its aim is to help you think and act like a pro.

The amateur lacks strategy. The pro is strategy positive. The difference between success and failure in the multi-family investing arena can be boiled down to a single juxtaposition: amateur vs. professional.

Too many investors want professional-level success without taking professional action execution, demeanor, mindset and systems. These all require strategy. Turning pro requires strategy.

Well-executed strategy breeds staying power, and staying power is sexy.

Have you ever been successful with a single-family portfolio? Great, but you can throw that experience away because – while the amateur approach works well enough over a small to medium sized portfolio of single-family properties, it won't get you far in the multi-family realm.

The amateur approach doesn't scale. You'll find out why in the next chapters.

To build legacy, to automate, to live freedom, and to make a difference, the multi-family investor must turn pro. Becoming a professional doesn't mean finding oneself a new full time job in real estate. It's a matter of strategic vision and strategic execution. There is no other path to the real estate promised land.

This will be our discussion.

But, what is specifically at stake here? What are the benefits of transitioning from amateur to professional? A strategic, well-executed professional multi-family investor can expect the following:

- Steady flow of investment capital
- Wealth growth (equity and cash flow)
- Improved lifestyle (no more late night toilet calls)
- Lowered chance of divorce (seriously)
- Staying power
- Legacy

Setting Some Terminology

Before we get into the meat of this book we must set a few rules of engagement. There are some basic assumptions and terms you need to understand.

Three distinct phases of real estate investing:

1. **Acquisition:** The all-important first stage. Too often, this task is done without as much as a nod to strategy or a clear picture of the real estate lifecycle. In this book, I will encourage you to be strategic about every multi-family building acquisition and to improve with each purchase.

2. **Optimization:** Usually, this is what you do during the first few months of investment ownership. It consists of operational changes and strategic renovations/changes. Lacking strategy and taking an ad hoc approach to the optimization phase is a sure path to mediocrity and perhaps erosion of staying power. Top-notch investors take this phase as seriously as the acquisition phase.

3. **Disposition:** We usually think of disposition as a sale, but in this book it might also mean continuing to own the asset. The decision whether or not to keep an asset is another strategic choice that requires understanding how the decision to keep one property may require the sale of others. Very few investors in the early stages of a career think this far ahead, but I will suggest thinking through to the disposition is vital to the development of staying power.

Please note that investors can be (and often are) in each of these three phases at the same time. We don't have the luxury of only thinking about only one of these at a time, but chances are you will be more involved in one of these phases than the others at any given time.

If we only think in one phase at a time we put ourselves at risk of losing the overall picture of the interaction between the three phases. We risk forgetting strategy. Real estate investing happens in the real world, so the relationship between things is more important than the things in isolation.

Have you ever noticed that the fastest runners in the world are never the best soccer players? Neither do you find the top high jumpers also the best basketball players, and the top scientists aren't usually the best leaders or CEOs. More complicated fields of expertise have more variables and require an understanding of the relationships between things. This can be hard for us to accept if we've been too heavily schooled. In school we are taught that the thing itself (a single subject or achieving a certain grade) is what's important. There is almost no emphasis placed on our ability to see relationships between things.

In the real world this is a valuable skill. In real estate investing it's the key skill of strategic success. So, while there are three distinct phases, I'm compelled to tell you that you must consider each phase as it relates to each other. This means thinking about optimization when buying, thinking about buying again when in disposition, etc.

Each phase informs the others at all times.

Let's move onto the next clarification:

There Are Three Types of Multi-Family Investor.

1. **Amateur Investors:** We all start as amateurs. If you're reading this book, there's a good chance you're an amateur investor on your path to becoming a professional. The thrust of this book is to help you develop the strategic approach required to become a professional.

   I've met amateur investors with 50 doors, and I know pro investors with one or two doors. If I had to bet which investor would be around in 10 years, I would bet on the pro with two doors over the amateur with 50 anytime.

   Chaos multiplies stress and disperses wealth. Strategy eliminates stress and concentrates wealth.

2. **Professional Investors:** Professionals have firmly planted their legacy or at least their ability to achieve a legacy.

   Professionals institute a series of actions that promote staying power. They understand the relationship between things, and know that success in the game is about more than just getting rich.

   Professionals take a strategic approach to every stage of the investment cycle. They think big picture and execute on strategy.

3. **Institutional Investors:** Institutional investors are high-level strategic operators. At this level, specialists are employed for detailed analyses and analytics that are not generally available to professional or amateur investors. We can learn a lot from institutional investors. Our actions become better by mirroring some of their behaviors.

   Institutional investors carry out acquisition, optimization, and disposition with pedantic consistency. The rest of us (amateurs and pros) may not be able to do so as consistently. We can model our behavior after institutional investors, and find greater levels of legacy building success as a result.

   It might sound like institutional investors have an unfair advantage over the rest of us, but their massive scale and enormous capital reserves also cause inefficiencies, which create opportunities ideal for smaller professional investors.

Build Staying Power

As with the three phases of the investment process, there is much room for crossover here. It might be that an investor is mostly a professional while continuing one amateur practice. Or, perhaps an investor is mostly amateur with one pro-level skill. This is how sales superstars grow weak portfolios without systems (we see this often). They have a pro-level ability to sell (and therefore raise investment capital), but they can't operate on a professional level across the rest of their business.

	Acquisition	Optimization	Disposition
Amateur	Buys randomly; thinks of cash flow and appreciation; unclear niche; overly broad niche; perhaps overly cautious (suffering) analysis paralysis	Waits for appreciation; renovates when something is broken; with no niche doesn't optimize operations well	Sells to get cash; doesn't use existing asset to 'niche-up'; fails to do tax planning before sale

Apartment Buildings That Outperform

	Acquisition	Optimization	Disposition
Professional	Has well defined niche; buys within niche wherever possible; is opportunistic when needed; tilts playing field within niche – every agent knows he/she is a buyer	Optimizes all buildings systematically; positions to capitalize on rare land and zoning optimization opportunities; reaps the rewards of niche in optimization activities	Doesn't necessarily think of the disposition as a sale; uses momentum from disposition to deepen within the niche; plans capital expenses to coincide with year of sale to improve NOI and valuation
Institutional	Buying is routine; most buying opportunities come to them as they are the biggest in niche; large niche to fit large business; positions niche for operational benefit (not just future appreciation)	May be a value-growth company or a wealth preservation company; optimization driven by data; leading edge tech advantages; optimizes by economy of scale	Timely sales for purpose of balance sheet; refinances at unbeatable interest rates; deepens ownership of niche with each disposition

Develop Staying Power

Staying power is the result of solid strategic planning and execution. Which specific strategies should real estate investors employ? These strategies are the 'meat and potatoes' of this book. Let's take a look at the strategies required for turning pro.

First, you will need a *legacy strategy*.

This is in sharp contrast to the non-strategy of so many early stage investors. You know what I'm talking about, right? I'm talking about the investors that think 'getting rich' or 'financial freedom' constitute a legacy strategy. They believe that income replacement is equal to legacy.

At best, these lofty ideals are goals. They're both non-specific and overly specific and miss the point, which is why they're not even good as goals. These goals are no substitution for a legacy strategy, which relates to family, society, knowing yourself and where you came from, and being fully conscious of where you're going. A legacy strategy starts with what's most important.

A legacy strategy can be described in a few steps:

1. **Envision:** where do you want real estate investing to take you in terms of:
    a. Assets and dollars
    b. What you will do with the assets and dollars
    c. How you will play the game

Yes, I'm telling you that real estate success is just as much about how you play the game as the monetary result. If you don't believe me, consider the legacies of Lance Armstrong, Ben Johnson and Charles Ponzi. They all played to win, but they are left with legacies I'm sure they didn't want. Real estate is full of those that get in for the wrong reasons. They falsely assume they can make a quick buck and get out.

Now to kill a myth: playing the game right doesn't take any more time than doing it wrong.

The legacy investor doesn't necessarily spend any more time or energy on his investments, but he or she uses them as a vehicle for good within the family, for him or herself, and within the community. The legacy investor understands from the start that these things are interconnected.

I'm not suggesting you define yourself by real estate success. I'm suggesting you will earn a legacy in any case, so ask yourself very clearly what you want that legacy to be. Once you decide, you can go after it with clarity and purpose.

In chapter 1 I will urge you to use your future legacy as the basis for your entire strategic approach.

Second, you will need a *niche strategy*.

Trying to be everything to everyone is the fastest path to mediocrity. Even the biggest players in the multi-family investing world focus on a niche. True, their niche might be a lot bigger than your niche, but they still have a niche. Apple makes electronics. They don't make tables, motorcycles or hair products. Coca-Cola makes a unique kind of sugar water. They don't deliver pizza.

The smaller we are as a business entity, the more focused our niche must be. Yet, most amateur real estate investors have this equation backwards. They think because they're small they can't afford to niche.

I'm going to suggest multi-family investors make their niche hyper-focused yet remain flexible enough to ensure they meet acquisition targets. If forced to buy outside of their niche to meet acquisition targets, investors should use the outside-niche asset as a lever to 'niche up'[1] by repositioning (a Solidifying Strategy).

Staying power comes with a strong niche focus.

The niche strategy is the central concept of this book. Being niched is a requirement for becoming a successful multi-family real estate investor, but the niche strategy isn't simple.

The most successful investors I know practice this niche strategy religiously, even if they don't know that this is what they're doing. The niche strategy is a complex movement that happens over multiple years, and if it's done well, it exponentially increases staying power.

---

[1] "Niche-up" is a term that will be used throughout this book. It means it means taking an opportunity to strengthen one's position in a given niche. Niching-up will be discussed in more detail in the section on the Solidifying Strategy.

Let's take a look at the movement-over-time of the niche strategy:

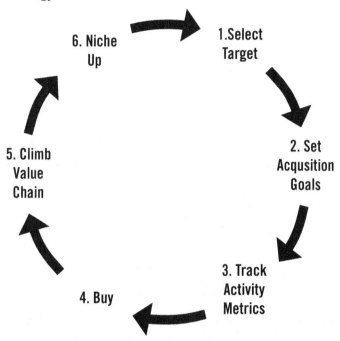

By employing a strong niche strategy, a multi-family investor transforms his or her business. There is no aspect of real estate investing that isn't improved by having a well-defined niche. Let's take a look at some of the benefits:

1. **Acquisition Simplicity:** By having a clearly defined niche, multi-family investors create buying opportunities. Focus allows us to become known as buyers of a specific property. Thus, we position ourselves in the minds of sellers and real estate agents as *the buyer* of a certain property type. Deals land on our doorstep that would otherwise go elsewhere.

2. **Operations Simplicity:** Have you ever tried to maintain two households at the same time? Then you'll know how much work this can be. Many people experience this every summer when they use a recreational property in addition to their home.

   Mowing two sets of lawns and painting two decks is more of a pain in the butt than we first expect.

   The same type of problem arises when trying to run multi-family operations across separate niches. Properties in the same niche have the same needs. Thus, we can streamline operations, but it's difficult to do this across multiple niches.

2. **Marketing and Branding:** Smaller investors don't often think of themselves as having a brand. This is important if an investor wants to become a professional.

   The purpose of a brand is to reduce resistance to sale. A brand is a product or service that occupies a certain place in the mind of a certain buyer. Imagine if Coke didn't have a brand position in your mind. Picture a Coke salesman trying to close you on purchasing a Coke, "It's a great drink. It's black and very sweet. Here give it a try!"

   Why do so many people (myself included) routinely pay double the price to buy Apple computers? Apple has a brand that occupies a position in our minds. There's Apple and then there's 'all the others'. The brand speaks to excellence, design and style. Buying an Apple feels like joining a special club (some would say cult).

How would you like to be the Apple of your limited sphere? You can, but it's only possible with a well-planned and executed niche strategy.

In our chapter on niche strategy we will discuss these benefits in greater detail. Furthermore, we will elaborate what constitutes a niche (and how to select one).

Third, you need an *optimization strategy*.

Think of each property as a chain. When you buy a property you grab hold of one end of the chain. Your purchase is aimed at undervalued or underperforming properties. Through the optimization phase you raise the value of that property by increasing the income, reducing the expenses, or changing the use. Once you've raised the value as high as possible you've reached the top of the value chain.

Here's a high-level view of potential optimization activities:

1. **Renovations:** Pro multi-family investors buy knowing they will constantly be renovating. This is the well-trodden path to moving up the value chain, and every active real estate investor must learn how to renovate early and often. We must be strategic about renovations to optimize best.

2. **Operations:** The least sexy component of multi-family real estate investing is operations. We love to hate it and we even deride it as, 'toilets and tenants.'

   Operational effectiveness makes or breaks real estate investors every day. A well-run operation is more important than the idea that you 'make money when you buy'. You risk losing it all if your operations aren't efficient, consistent, and aligned with your business model.

There is more to operations than just management, too. Bookkeeping, marketing, and branding are all part of the equation. This is a vital component of moving up the value chain.

3. **Land and Zoning:** Some of the best value-add opportunities are hidden within a building's land and zoning. By understanding the land and zoning of your assets (before and during ownership) you have the opportunity to move up the value chain – scratch that – you have the opportunity to add links to the value chain by changing the use, adding to the building, or providing more opportunities to future owners. Such is the scope of land and zoning opportunities.

We will discuss each of these in detail in the optimization section.

Fourth, you will need a *solidifying strategy*.

Once you reach the top of the value chain you will have some strategic decisions to make because the top of the value chain is when to employ a solidifying strategy, which often requires repositioning.

Remember, we're not talking about stocks, so there are several ways to profit in real estate beyond just cashing out. In real estate, there is every chance that the investor may do better by not selling.

Remember, our goal is *legacy*, not necessarily pure profit. Solidifying your holdings will make your portfolio more stable, more profitable, and easier to manage. In addition, it will make you more focused on enjoying the benefits of the optimization you've created.

Let's take a quick look at a few of the top-of-the-chain solidifying choices:

1. **Sell and Reposition:** Knowing that long-term success comes from solidifying one's niche, an investor that has reached the top of a value chain has a unique opportunity to use one asset as a pawn to strengthen his or her central position.

   In the board game Monopoly you trade in four houses for a hotel. The same principle applies here.

2. **Refinance:** At the top of the value-chain the property may be optimized. In order to solidify, the investor might need to execute a refinance prior to keeping the property for the long haul.

3. **Keep as is:** Doing nothing is sometimes a more potent strategic move than doing something. The professional investor knows this and at the right times chooses to do nothing instead of something.

In our solidifying strategy chapter we will discuss the various components a multi-family investor must consider to solidify his or her position and build staying power.

Taking Action

The purpose of this introduction has been to share a vision of your future with you. We've been having fun, haven't we? I hope you enjoyed it because it's time to get serious.

Please don't do what most people do, which is to read a book packed with useful information, then put it on a shelf and forget about it. You're reading this book because you're ready to take the next step in your real estate investment career, so let me ask you a question:

What would have happened if you never took action in other areas of life?

If you're here, it means you've likely tried your hand at single family investing, and since it worked, you've decided to take the next step.

Or, you haven't started investing in real estate yet, but you're reading this book to learn about the professional investors' habits and strategic approach before beginning a career in real estate investment.

Either way, I have to warn you against finishing this book and putting it away on the shelf. Such a non-action is death to professionalism. Here's why: *the true mark of a professional is the habit of taking action.* It comes before strategy, before execution, before professional relationships.

This book is packed with multi-family investing wisdom, but to capitalize on the wisdom you must take immediate and consistent action. The first step is to turn the page right now and begin reading the 'meat and potatoes' of this book. Get started now. Don't waste any more time.

CHAPTER 1
The Legacy Strategy

> "No legacy is so rich as honesty."
>
> – William Shakespeare

Start from the Right Place

The hallmark of strategic thinking is advanced vision. It's not that we believe the future will look exactly as we envision. Such prescience is impossible and things never look exactly as we imagined. We need to be pointing in the right direction from the start in order to end up where we want to be.

Let's call such forward thinking *a legacy vision*, which is in sharp contrast to a *get-rich-quick vision*.

Those with a get-rich-quick vision run from deal-to-deal and can't articulate their 'why' beyond making money or replacing their income. People with get-rich-quick visions leave messy legacies.

A legacy vision isn't about goals or even a positive mindset – not that goals are bad, but legacy vision is deeper than goal setting. Goals can help put targets around activity, but amateurs seem to define themselves by goals. When they ask, "who am I?" the response is, "I'm a person that has the goal to purchase a thousand doors."

This is not a legacy approach.

Attachment to goals causes us to ignore the larger question of who we are becoming in the process. Goals can orient us away from what really matters. One hundred units becomes the purpose for existing. This is perverse, because it's just a number. It only has meaning because we give it meaning, yet there are things in the world that have meaning beyond our selfish justifications.

So, you have 100 units. Well, that's great. If vacancy goes up by four per cent would you be able to stay in business? Many get-rich-quick types would have to say no (if they were being honest). Plenty of real estate rising stars get wiped out every time the market takes a tumble because they don't invest with legacy in mind. In fact, 'rising star' isn't even an apt metaphor. They're more like fireworks than a rising stars because they burn out so quickly. This quick burn is caused by the lack of a legacy foundation. It's a failure to focus beyond the limited profit-taking mindset.

The First Type of Legacy: The Success Legacy

To understand legacy better, we have to break it down into the two separate streams. First, there is *success legacy*, which is what most people think of when they consider the benefits of real estate.

It's the kind of legacy that allows you to pay for your child's post-secondary education or take your family on a yearlong Caribbean sailing adventure, as one Edmonton investing family did.

Imagine getting on an airplane when the Canadian winter is settling in and heading off to the Caribbean to hop islands with your family. Imagine teaching your kids about biology on a beach or math by shopping in multiple currencies. This is legacy enabled by real estate. It's being able to provide something that only wealth can provide.

Philanthropy is another common type of *success legacy*. Many people dream of philanthropic activities, and it's a strong driving motivation for many investors.

Many working people have just enough money to pay the bills, a bit for retirement, and a couple of hundred dollars here and there for philanthropic causes. People quickly learn that their small contributions don't make as big of a difference as they'd like. This feeling drives many people into investing, as they want to create a legacy of philanthropy.

I love this success legacy motivation.

It reminds me of a man I once met when travelling through British Columbia. He had built up a successful portfolio of real estate, and in addition to being able to live on an oceanfront property up the coast from Vancouver (success legacy), he and his wife were also committed philanthropists.

He told me about a time when a local councillor was about to lose his job due to government cutbacks. He explained that he believed in the work the councillor was doing, so he donated money to pay the youth councillor's salary and keep him working. "My son got into a couple of scrapes when he was 15, and the youth councillor helped get him back on track. I wanted to make sure he could keep doing his job," he said.

This man could never have been this kind of philanthropist without the additional wealth created through real estate investing success.

Success legacy looks different for everyone.

For some it looks like only working three-hour days for life rather than 10-hour days. For others, a success legacy might be about helping set up a younger relative on an early path to financial security, as my friend Russell Westcott did.

A few years back he registered his niece as one-quarter owner of one of his cash-flowing properties. She'll get firsthand experience on the value of investing, the good and the bad.

These are all examples of success legacy.

The Second Type of Legacy: The Action Legacy

The second kind of legacy is the *action legacy*. It's based on a simple principle: the acquisition of wealth is not worth the pain of another person. Building wealth through real estate is a noble goal. However, it's not okay when your own wealth comes at the cost of another's wellbeing.

First, do no harm.

It sounds simple, but achieving an action legacy is a bit trickier than one might think. For example, Andrew Carnegie famously gave away his enormous wealth. In fact, he had the stated goal of dying penniless, believing that it was wrong to hoard wealth and that it was his duty to put his fortune back into the common good.

His was a classic (and extreme) example of a success legacy vision based on philanthropy. Keep in mind that if Carnegie's wealth were translated into today's dollars it would be nearly five times greater than Bill Gates's current wealth. We're talking about a lot of money, and he gave it all away.

Nobody can doubt Carnegie's *success legacy*. But, Carnegie was also known for the (sometimes ruthless) treatment of the workers in his factories, even going so far as to authorize a top manager of one of his steel mills to commit violence against workers attempting to organize a union. For this reason, Carnegie's legacy is sometimes questioned (although it should be noted that at other times he was a great champion of workers).

Did his accumulation of wealth, which he then recycled back into society, end up being a greater good than the death and harm his company's actions caused to the workers that made him rich?

It's a difficult question to answer.

Let's think of it another way: what if, rather than accumulating the equivalent of $300 billion, he only

Apartment Buildings That Outperform

accumulated $150 billion, but in doing so improved the treatment of his employees and enriched thousands of them at the same time? That's a lot of workers who would've been able to purchase homes, pay for children's education, and cycle the money back into society.

The libraries and universities are great, but wouldn't the extra money in the economy have done a greater good? Which legacy would have been greater? Would he then still be known as one of the "Robber Barons"? Would his actions have influenced Rockefeller and the other Robber Barons?

These are impossible questions to answer. My only point in bringing them up is that there are daily business actions we can take that improve our odds of securing our action legacy.

Many never consider this side of legacy, partially because of the persistent myth that business success requires others to suffer. If you believe this myth you might want to consider what is going to be left of your heart and soul after a lifetime of such activity.

Time after time, business owners, entrepreneurs, and investors realize only after it's too late that the way they carry themselves in business outweighs any success they may have garnered.

If you don't believe me, ask yourself if you've ever seen a rich, lonely man driving a luxury car, living alone (divorced) in an expensive home that his kids refuse to visit. It happens all the time. In my life my faith and my relationships come before financial success. Having it the wrong way around ensures a negative legacy.

The Legacy Strategy

What is the point of all this work, anyways? You and I could stick to a normal job and avoid the hard work, stress, and difficult decisions that come with real estate investing.

Unless you're in it for a legacy of positive change there is no reason to be in it. Positive change happens within individual people who then spread that change to the world around them.

Investors create legacy when they stand in front of a tenant, treating them as equals, fully aware of and compassionate to their unique circumstance. Every time an investor says, "Oh well, it's too inconvenient to fix that problem," at the expense of a tenant, they create a negative legacy. I will argue that this kind of negative legacy can and does outweigh whatever an investor is trying to create on the success legacy side.

You know who does things that way? Amateurs. Pros are aware that they can't reach the top at the expense of others. They know they can be conscientious and that every action they take creates a ripple effect in the world.

Pros know they can be profit-focused while improving the world through their every action, building legacy with each step. The most successful people I know consider their work as service. They believe they have a sacred duty to carry out right action in their daily lives, for the betterment of the whole.

I will mention Boardwalk Rental Communities (Boardwalk for short) several times throughout this book because they are an example of a successful real estate investment company that should be emulated on many levels, though not without their own mistakes, but with great lessons about *success legacy* and *action legacy*.

A couple of years ago Boardwalk instituted an impressive policy, which I first learned about during an Edmonton Apartment Association meeting. The policy states that no individual Boardwalk tenant will have his or her rent raised by more than $150 in any given year.

If you're cynical, you could say this is just posturing and smart positioning, nothing more than good PR. It may be these things, but I'm okay with PR that puts a company on solid moral ground, so long as they act in accordance with their public statements. This policy protects thousands of people, and it has helped Boardwalk create an action legacy.

Boardwalk also does mission trips to Mexico where they give back to the less fortunate. This is a company with over 600 employees and tens of thousands of tenants. They even bring some of their tenants on the yearly mission trip (along with some employees).

Boardwalk is focused on a *success legacy* as well as an *action legacy*. In fact, it's a great example of the two types of legacy combined in one business. Everyone from ownership, to employees, to tenants shares the same goals.

I'm not suggesting a small investor could have the same size impact as a company of Boardwalk's size, but the principle is sound and can be used in any size of operation.

Another example of action legacy on a smaller (but not insignificant) scale is my Edmonton investing compatriot,

Jeff Gunther. Jeff is a focused and successful investor, who is oriented towards both types of legacy.

Jeff's focused niche is three-bedroom townhouses that cater to young families. Within his niche, he has a simple goal of standardizing every unit he owns so that he charges an average rent while maintaining the property at an above average standard.

He wants the tenants of these properties to feel 'slightly uncomfortable' that the property was a little *too nice*. This is only half-joking, as many of the tenants do feel uncomfortable for a brief time.

This might sound weird, but the slight discomfort turns into *feeling valued* very quickly. Imagine that for a moment. Here are people that have become accustomed to landlords that don't care, and just by delivering an outstanding product at a standardized price-point Jeff is able to make a real difference.

Don't tell me real estate investors can't create outstanding legacies.

Jeff's goal is to elevate the quality of rentals for his niche. It's an action legacy. Generations of families' lives will be improved by raising this rental standard. The only way this world gets better is by individuals taking action. As investors, we have a special opportunity to make a difference.

Now, Jeff doesn't stop there. He is now acquiring and constructing rental units throughout the city. On one hand, this is a business strategy. Keep in mind that there has been no significant multi-family rental buildings constructed for several decades. This makes his construction of multi-family buildings a legacy action, too.

Make no mistake – Jeff wouldn't be building these rental units if they weren't profitable. Nobody wins if he goes out of business, but keep in mind that he had a choice. He could have developed condos units for sale and likely made more money, but Jeff is driven by legacy. He wants to make money of course, but he also wants his business to be a vehicle for good.

Building affordable housing does that.

Contrast Jeff's legacy vision with that of a big-time commercial real estate broker I met not long ago[2]. He assured me that his (and his firm's) goal was to 'rule the world'. I politely thanked him for the coffee, but that idea does not align with the way I work and I don't want to be part of such a legacy. This is a person who would be unlikely to pass up a few dollars. I'll take Jeff's legacy over his any day.

Achieving both types of legacy (success and action) require strategic focus. You won't be sailing the Caribbean or undertaking philanthropic endeavors if you can't thrive in the good times and survive in the bad.

---

2   In the commercial real estate brokerage world there's a lot of recruiting done over a friendly coffee. Was a job offer going to be coming from this meeting? I don't know but as I've reflected on it I'm glad it didn't. They're doing great business but I'm not sure the personal fit was there.

Furthermore, you, your tenants, business partners, and your team will not be able to benefit by your action unless you maintain pro-level execution. Legacy through action is a natural result of focus.

> ### Temple Grandin – Legacy through Compassion
>
> Temple Grandin is a world famous industrial designer, professor and author. She's also one of the most eloquent and convincing voices demystifying autism in the world today. She rose to prominence by becoming one of the world's foremost experts on (and advocates for) the humane treatment of animals – especially farm animals.
>
> She has revolutionized the treatment of animals in slaughterhouses and feedlots through animal-friendly designs of handling facilities and equipment. Temple is unique in that the secret to her success is compassion.
>
> You see, her unique view of the world (and high level of affinity for animals) have turned out to be a huge advantage for her, the animals she's helped, and clients she's served. Putting herself (literally) in the dirt with the cattle in a feedlot, she's identified the stressful areas of cattle handling facilities. Her clients (the smart ones) have implemented the changes she suggested. In doing so, they have profited and their animals have suffered much less.
>
> Everyone wins.

She would literally get down to the level of the cattle chutes and see all of the potential stress points for the cattle. She has left a legacy of animal welfare, improved working conditions, and improved operations for the owners of the feedlots. – All because she was able to apply compassion for animals.

Today, many of the high-density cattle and pig handling facilities in North America are Grandin's designs. This has resulted in far less stress and suffering for the animals handled in her facilities, more profit for the owners of the facilities (as there are fewer animal accidents), and better conditions for the workers handling the animals.

Like Temple Grandin, you will also have to act with compassion to secure an action legacy. How does your decision affect your team? How does it affect your renters? How does it affect the community? Do you get down in the dirt?

Just to reiterate: I am not suggesting you do any of this at the expense of your bottom line, but *I am* suggesting you pay attention to others' needs. Your bottom line does not come before another's well-being.

If you think through problems from the vantage point of others, just as Temple Grandin did for animals, then you will be assured of leaving a great action legacy behind.

CHAPTER 2
The Niche Strategy

> *"Trying to get everyone to like you is a sign of mediocrity."*
>
> Colin Powell

Directly Indirect

One of the realities of business is that we have to make choices about whom we can serve, and trying to please everyone is the path to mediocrity. I'm not sure if it's our desire to be liked or our misunderstanding of the power of a niche, but many (probably most) real estate investors never develop a niche. Instead they select and hold property randomly and un-strategically.

On the other hand, there are investors who were once niche-focused but fell prey to hubris along the way and lost their niche focus.

If you're old enough you will remember when the Coca-Cola Corporation launched "New Coke," which was an unmitigated disaster, as the company turned their back on their niche. The people who loved Coca-Cola were incensed. They didn't want change. Coca-Cola represented tradition and a perfect recipe. Changing just to meet the threat of Pepsi's upstart marketing efforts represented Coca-Cola's turning its back on its niche.

It reminds me of a successful multi-family investor in my home market of Edmonton (let's call her Diane) who lost focus, and it nearly cost her entire portfolio. She had been successful investing in her niche (Edmonton west-end multi-family) for many years, but she eventually decided to speed up expansion and start buying in new markets, not just new parts of town, but new markets altogether.

In theory, this made a lot of sense. Edmonton prices had been rising. There were fewer buying opportunities remaining in Edmonton. Meanwhile, there were other markets that still remained fundamentally sound. Due to her past successes, Diane was bringing in a lot of capital at this time, and she thought she'd never be able to put it all to work in Edmonton. Thus, she turned her eyes outward.

Theoretically, it made sense. Diane found markets with better fundamentals and strong cash flow. The only thing that didn't make sense was that her new acquisition phase broke a cardinal rule – to follow the niche strategy.

As usually happens when a business tries to expand too fast, Diane soon learned that entering a single new market requires a high-level of involvement, building new teams, due diligence. Basically, every component of the business needs to start from scratch.

The Niche Strategy

When entering a new niche (on the occasion it is actually a good idea) it's always best to move laterally into a niche very near the original one. If you're targeting a demographic or a specific geographical need, try to replicate it. Just as a conquering army first controls its own territory before it conquers its neighbor. The army doesn't rush to a faraway land to conquer before first defeating its own neighbour.

It's like trying to hold Asia in the board game Risk – you receive seven extra men at the beginning of every turn, but all those extra 'assets' don't often help because you're spread so thin.

Just as supply lines get longer and defenses get weaker the further an army extends, so does the investor's ability to properly manage her assets and to have a solid understanding of what's happening on the ground.

Diane's new acquisitions seemed perfectly situated for long-term growth across varied markets in North America. But small problems piled up, and she found she could never quite replicate the initial success of her home niche. Every new market brought a new challenge, and every challenge was unique to the new market. In a couple of cases, the combined effect of the small problems resulted in big problems.

Luckily, Diane is a plucky investor, and she realized just in time that she was overextended. Supply lines were strained, and she knew she had to bring the troops home. Perhaps if she'd been conscious of how many new niches she was trying to exploit, then she'd have been more cautious.

Diane's story shows that the niche choices investors make when acquiring real estate are choices they have to live with for a long time. It takes time and effort to build a strong presence in a great niche, but it only takes a couple of missteps to weaken one's niche strategy.

Just as an army embroiled in a conflict overseas is weakened at home, so is an investor stretched thin across multiple niches. Of course, Diane's story is somewhat extreme. She bought in cities all around North America. Not all investors go that far outside of a focused niche, but many lose their niche focus even in their same geographical region. Shiny objects distract too many investors.

The opposite and by far more effective method is to be strategic about niche. Of course, there is a risk of becoming too cautious by overthinking these niche selections. I'm not suggesting that you strategize yourself into a corner. There is room to make (small) buying mistakes. Buying not-quite-perfect properties for your niche is far better than buying nothing. Successful investors know they won't get it right 100 per cent of the time, and they will re-position their portfolio where necessary.

Action must be taken, but there is huge advantage to buying strategically with operations (and indeed the exit) in mind. The change in indirect factors is unique to each area. It challenges operations and creates opportunity with respect to competition. There are unique operational challenges in each niche (geographic and demographic). In the rush to expand, many investors forget that each niche has a unique texture (and indeed each building has a unique texture). These unique textures create opportunity against competition.

When investors lose their niche focus it's usually because they get addicted to the cash flow they create during optimization without realizing that now is the time to dispose of the property, pull out some value and reposition the equity into another property that's more closely aligned with their niche.

After a couple of years of high-stress and stagnating profit, Diane realized that the effort of buying in all the far-flung locales wasn't worth the reward. She finally refocused, sold where necessary, and put her efforts into solidifying her niche.

Today, her company is enjoying the benefits of focus. She buys one type of property, in one type of neighborhood, with one type of tenant. Rather than chasing deals, they come to her with seemingly no effort.

Important: it only *seems* like no effort. Diane has put in years of groundwork to become a known investor in her niche. This is why people bring her deals. She's established in her niche, and it took a lot of work. It takes time to establish a niche and the rewards come later.

If you're a relative newcomer, Diane's problem might seem like a high-class problem to have. It was her success that enabled her to expand her business to distant locations. Don't be fooled. This can and does happen to investors all the time – even smaller investors.

Investors spread across two or more niches find themselves doing everything twice (or more). Two buildings in the same niche can share the same advertising, onsite manager, and much more. They derive the benefit of good word of mouth advertising if they're positioned to capture the same demographic. Two buildings in separate niches, even within the same city, require a duplication of effort on all fronts.

The steps of the niche strategy can be laid out as follows:

1. **Find a Target Niche:** With a thorough yet rapid analysis, the pro investor chooses a specialized niche that makes sense. This niche must be big enough to ensure enough buying opportunities yet small enough to be a specialized.

2. **Acquisition:** The investor finds deals, writes offers, and purchases property. They have a strong awareness of how closely the properties align to their niche and how effectively they'll be able to add value.

3. **Normalize/Optimize:** During this period, the investor gains additional insight into their property and target niche. Based on the feedback from being in the trenches, the investor will gain a better understanding of whether or not an individual property fits the target niche, or if the target niche requires adjustment.

4. **Disposition/Reposition:** Based on the real-time feedback, the investor makes strategic decisions whether or not to keep as is, sell, or refinance a property.

The following sections will discuss the details that go into niche selection. Read on to find out how to dominate a multi-family investing niche.

Benefits of Niche Specialization

Lacking a strong niche focus can be deadly to real estate investors, and it has proven to be the undoing of plenty of unfocused real estate investors. Let's take a look at some of the benefits of being niche focused:

1. **Acquisition:** Being niche-focused starts working for the multi-family investor from the beginning of the ownership process. Rather than looking for 'a building' you look for a specific type of building that will be tenanted by a specific type of tenant in a specific neighborhood.

   Acquisition gets easier with each property as you become clearer and your reputations as a player in your niche grows.

   Many investors fear that by choosing a tight niche they will not have acquisition options. Later, I will show you a simple formula for ensuring your niche is big enough to support your vision.

2. **Branding:** By working a specific niche you allow yourself the opportunity to develop a brand. Brands are attached to a specific product. The more specific the product, the clearer the brand is in the prospect's mind.

   Imagine the branding opportunity if your niche was a 25-block radius in a single neighborhood. The same people that live in one building in the neighborhood will have friends and family in similar buildings in the same neighborhood. They tell each other things.

A brand is born in the simple act of one friend telling another, "My landlord is great, and he has more suites available like this one." You will never have this opportunity without a niche.

> *"People influence people. Nothing influences people more than a recommendation from a trusted friend. A trusted referral influences people more than the best broadcast message."*
>
> **- Mark Zuckerberg (Facebook Founder)**

There is no better, more consistent, and historically effective way to remove resistance to sale than by referrals. How is one tenant supposed to refer friends and family to your building unless they know that another building is yours?

Having four buildings spread out across four different niches does not allow you this opportunity. You will never gain the benefit of a brand (removing resistance to sale) without first positioning in a niche.

2. **Marketing:** Marketing vacancies can be a time-consuming and costly process each time a property comes up for rent. Or it can be simple, consistent, targeted and effective.

The Niche Strategy

The choice is yours, but you only receive the benefits of marketing simplicity once established in a niche. Imagine an investor with one property well-suited for military people in the northeast corner of the city, another tailor-made for nurses in the southwest, and a third perfect for downtown hipsters. Such an investor will never reap the benefit of marketing simplicity because each of these niches requires a separate marketing approach.

There are niche-dominating multi-family investment companies whose marketing seems like the *only option* for their niches. They have become synonymous with the niche, and whether tenants like it or not, they must at least consider the company when apartment shopping in their niche. They appear to be everywhere because every penny of marketing effort is aimed in the same direction.

These niche-dominators don't advertise 'a suite' for rent. Instead, they advertise suites for rent, at all times, knowing that they will always have one or two available. When the tenant comes looking they have several properties to choose from.

In addition, these niche-dominators create waiting lists, and they market newly available suites to their database of existing and past tenants. Much of their marketing is nearly free, since it's much cheaper to email all your tenants than to pay for a newspaper ad.

3. **Renovating:** Just as investors achieve critical mass on marketing by having a niche focus so do they with renovations. Failing to have a niche focus means failing to capitalize on scales of economy when renovating.

   Renovations are continuous and ongoing – at least they should be, since a big part of strategic focus is to raise the value of a property with improvements in the optimization phase.

   Renovation standards must match tenant profiles. With properties scattered in different areas with different tenant profiles investors end up renovating with different materials and different methods. This causes problems with buying in bulk and keeping stock of the most often-used renovation materials such as paint and trim.

4. **Management:** One excellent onsite manager is worth his or her weight in antimatter (most valuable substance known to man). When servicing a tight geographic niche, investors can benefit from great onsite managers.

   Such managers help create community, familiarity, and comfort with the building and the people living there. The consistent presence of a knowledgeable onsite manager over the years is often a deciding factor of a building's success or failure.

   By having a solid niche, investor's support their invaluable onsite managers as they find tenants and do much of the brand-building work. Too many investors own a mish-mash of properties with no connecting link between one building and another. They expect their property managers to work miracles, when in truth the responsibility is on the owners to develop a niche strategy.

Now it's time to define the components of a niche. As we have hinted in this chapter, a niche is made up of two factors:

1. **Geography:** This might mean having buildings in close proximity with each other, or it might mean having buildings that aren't in proximity but share geographical similarities. This factor will be discussed in Chapter 3, along with the two sub-requirements:

    a. **Transportation Nodes:** People live in a geographic niche if it fulfills their transportation needs.

    b. **Employment Nodes:** People will live in a geographic niche if they can fulfill their employment needs. Think of Silicon Valley in northern California. Smaller cities have their own version of geographically centralized employment nodes, too.

2. **Demographic:** Similar types of people tend to live in similar buildings. Targeting a niche is as much about the people as the neighbourhood. Having a solid understanding of the types of tenants one is seeking has many advantages. Demographics will be discussed in Chapter 4.

CHAPTER 3

Niche Strategy – Geography

> *"Why the hell would I drive across town when I'm not being paid to?"*
>
> Chris Davies

Macro Geography

The question of *where* is perhaps the most important factor considered by professional investors, but too many investors approach geography from only the economic viewpoint. Diane's story illustrates this fact well enough. She expanded based only on the economic potential of an area.

A macro-economic focus is important, but the best economics in the world won't save an investor where operations suffer, which can happen if a geographical region is chosen without regard to the overall picture.

Certainly, the macro is important. Choosing a city or town to invest in is no small decision, and no investor should make this choice lightly. Nobody wants to get stuck investing in a poorly performing city or town. Professional investors question common assumptions and follow the money. They invest where there will be strong demand for rental stock. They choose an investment town based on the economic fundamentals that drive the entire region.

However, to be strategic about geography, investors must also consider the micro, that is, the geography of the chosen target niche. 'Calgary multi-family buildings targeted towards working-class families and couples near a transit station' is a different geographic niche than 'Calgary multi-family'.

It's not enough to choose a geographic region based only on the economics. This would be failing to properly choose a niche. The Real Estate Investment Network (REIN), which I've been a member of for many years, provides investors with many remarkable insights into choosing the best geographic niche. The following is REIN's list of criterion for choosing a geographic region for investment:

- Is there an overall increase in demand?
- Sales over list?
- Increase in labour and materials cost?
- Speculative investment in the area?
- Area in transition?
- Transportation improvement?
- Short-term problem?
- Ripple effect?

- Overall inflation rate?
- Real Estate spring or summer?
- Political leadership created growth atmosphere?
- Average income increasing faster than average?
- Attractive to baby boomers?
- Higher than average migration?
- Interest rates at lows and moving downward?
- Can you use unique marketing to increase cash flow or value?
- Can you change the use of the property?
- Can you buy it substantially below retail market value?
- Can you substantially increase the rents?
- Can you do renovations to increase the value?

I won't discuss the economic factors in detail. REIN is the go-to Canadian source for real estate specific news and economics. I will focus on the geography insofar as it relates to developing a strong multi-family investing niche.

Concentration vs. Proximity in Choosing a Geographic Niche

Having a clear understanding of the macroeconomics of your investment region is a starting point. This is a requirement for playing the big-kid game of multi-family investing.

Suffice it to say you need to understand and be certain that your region will benefit from economic factors (not suffer) over the long haul. You must understand and apply this type of top-level thinking to behave like a professional multi-family investor. It's a mistake to think this knowledge is all you need to know about geography.

This is a common mistake of amateurs. They think, "Edmonton is a great investment town, so all I have to do is buy there and I'll be a great success." It's a solid economic region, but that doesn't make it a magical region. Investments will still underperform if investors don't behave strategically.

The rule for geography is: *always seek to concentrate your holdings.*

However, we must draw a distinction between concentration and proximity. Concentrating your holdings allows an investor to appeal to a particular demographic (and cohort). Similar types of people are attracted to similar areas, so having holdings concentrated enables demographic focus.

But, there are circumstances when concentrations of people don't live in proximity to one another. Similar types of people often live in disparate geographical areas of a city. Investors who are wise to this know that they can target a geographic niche that is *concentrated but not proximate.*

Renter demographics can be similar in all of their habits yet not live in geographic proximity. These individuals are similar but don't all live in the same neighbourhoods. An

Niche Strategy – Geography

investor can have a geographic niche yet still be spread out. Such a situation increases operational effort slightly, but since the same niche is still the focus, then much of the operational effort is still streamlined.

There is a Western Canadian investment company that epitomizes this approach (let's call them Company X). Company X has chosen the Generation Y demographic as a niche (much more on that later). More specifically, they've targeted Gen-Y renters that drive and likely work in the energy or construction industries. This is in contrast to the Gen-Y renters that don't drive and like to live in the densest parts of a city, usually downtown. Company X's target niche values mobility because to them it signifies independence.

This niche (Gen-Y workers that drive) has a high standard of living. They only rent a property that has a higher end condo feel that's convenient for their lifestyle. They work, have money and drive. Convenience and freedom means living close to a major thoroughfare for them.

This profile is perfectly suited for the newer suburbs that are within a stone's throw of an entrance/exit to a ring road. Saskatoon, Calgary, and Edmonton all have new ring roads, and this is where Company X has built its niche. The new ring roads in all three cities represent massive transportation developments with dozens of entry points.

Company X's holdings are not all close in proximity but are concentrated around a certain geographical feature in each city – namely an exit to a ring road. What's interesting is this company's units attract a lot of construction professionals. They advertise around NAIT (in Edmonton), which is next to downtown. This works because their target demographic is people that make a great salary out of trade school. For marketing purposes they capitalize on the geographic concentration of prospects in and around NAIT.

There is a saying that you may have heard, "Ignore fads but ride trends." There is a large cohort in Edmonton, Calgary, and Saskatoon of growing populations of young people that work in industry. This company is a great example of riding the trend of young, industry working people.[3] The cohort of these young construction and energy workers is also highly mobile, so they reap the benefits of consistent branding when their clients move from Edmonton to other areas like Saskatoon or Cold Lake. Their buildings, systems, paperwork and many personnel are the same, so it takes very little effort to keep a happy tenant in their network. Vacancies market themselves inside the ecosystem they've created.

Company X based its strategy on the macroeconomic trends for future growth, but for operations and branding success, they based their microeconomic strategy on a clear understanding of the difference between concentration and proximity. This enabled them to articulate a clear and successful niche strategy. Even though their holdings (in

---

3   This is a cohort that has high earning potential but is also linked to the energy and construction industries, both of which are fundamentally cyclical. It's an interesting gamble.

each city) aren't in the same neighbourhoods, they are *concentrated*, which allows them to profit from all of the benefits of niching.

Employment and Transportation Nodes

We already know that concentration doesn't always mean proximity, so what is the factor (or factors) that hold a geographical niche together?

It's useful to think of **employment nodes** and **transportation nodes** when developing a geographic niche.

The above example (Company X) is a case of taking advantage of both an employment node and a transportation node. Upwardly mobile, young, construction (and other) industry workers fulfills the employment node. Most of these jobs are either on Edmonton's outskirts or one of the surrounding industry towns like Nisku, Leduc, Fort Saskatchewan or Devon.

This renter type doesn't walk, ride a bike, or take the bus. They drive. A vehicle count in the parking lot of a Company X building at 10 p.m. would turn up a high number of pickup trucks. Being driver's means they want to live in an area that caters to their need to drive, so they choose to live near ring road entrance points. Thus, it's a transportation node.

Servicing this niche fulfills both nodes, which is perfect if you can do it. If not, then a single node will do. Often both nodes go hand in hand.

For example, consider the demographic shift to Edmonton's downtown, which is very much about getting more workers downtown, a place that was not in style for several generations in Edmonton.

The jobs are going back downtown, and the movement of people there is about an employment node. The whole idea of downtown density fulfills a transportation node by encouraging public transport, walking and bicycling.

Perhaps the largest demographic shift in Edmonton (and let's face it all across North America) is the other type of Gen-Y – those moving to the higher density parts of the city. We just finished discussing a cohort (more on that later) within Gen-Y that wants to live on the outskirts of prairie cities near ring roads, but the larger cohort within the Gen-Y demographic is to the downtown. Colloquially, we often identify this cohort as, 'hipsters'.

This process of downtown residential development is much farther along in Calgary, which is why there is such a high concentration of condos in downtown Calgary and near 17th Ave.

In Edmonton, many Gen-Y people take the LRT or a bus. They walk to get groceries, ride bikes in the summer and live as much of a car-free life as possible. This is new to Edmonton, a lifestyle that was traditionally impossible in the suburban sprawl. Living downtown is very much a transportation node based decision, just as it's an employment node based decision.

By studying the Edmonton trend, we can see that many jobs are moving downtown, while at the same time there's a separate movement of jobs going further away from the density. This movement is industry and property value based. These two opposing forces (people moving to density and away from the centre) are forming a split distribution of jobs in Edmonton.

The Two Nodes and Niche Viability

With so many Gen-Y people moving downtown, there are real estate sub-niches being formed. Simply choosing to service 'downtown Gen-Y' might be too broad now. So, how does an investor choose a sub-niche within a broader niche?

Investors need to be hyper-focused. Will you, as a new, or even as a moderately well-established multi-family real estate investor be able to compete with the institutional-level investors that own brand new 300-suite towers? You may not be able to compete head-to-head with them, but you may be able to service a niche they can't with their size.

Smaller investors risk being stuck below the big players in a niche that doesn't have enough properties to be viable. Hence, we need to discuss what makes a niche viable. Let's take a look at niche-viability through the lens of the different nodes.

Transportation Nodes

On the opposite end of the spectrum from downtown Gen-Y niche are the union-working blue-collar northeast Edmonton lifetime-renters. This tenant type is over 40, has a stable job driving a grader (or something similar) that pays them well enough. They have no delusions of grandeur or desire for upward mobility, but they aren't short on cash, either. Overall, they're great renters.

They have arrived, and they're not interested in style, hip music, lively debate, understanding trends, or anything else new and different. Breakfast is bacon, recreation is TV, and sports are religion.

Many investors hate this niche, but I love it. It's a wonderful niche once you adjust your expectations, which would involve looking for the right things as a real estate investor. For example, this tenant-type tends to smoke more than other tenant-types, which means they have few other housing options.

Once they move into a home they hate to leave.

This tenant type isn't usually into health or personal development, so as a rental incentive you will want to consider free pizza and beer rather than a health club membership.

Every city has this niche to a certain degree, as every city has blue-collar workers. Edmonton has several geographic areas with this niche because there are a high number of blue-collar workers in Edmonton.

Niche Strategy – Geography

The trick is how to capture this niche. Since it's large, one must focus down to one subset of this niche to maintain focus. This means setting geographical limitations. This way you will capture a specific sub-set of this niche.

Rather than just going after, 'blue-collar tenants', a proper niche would focus on properties only within 800 metres of Stadium, Coliseum, Belvedere, or Clareview LRT stations.

For those readers unfamiliar with Edmonton, these are the four stations north of the LRT line, which travels to the northeast, and have a large proportion of working-class tenants nearby.

However, there are several niches of working class people, each with different living situations. There are working class homeowners, working class condo-buyers, working class house renters, working class basement suite renters, and working class multi-family renters.

To niche down a sub-set below just 'working class', one must target a type of living situation (which you've already done by being in the multi-family game) and then solve a specific node.

An employment node in Edmonton could be working class house rentals around the refinery district. Apartment building within 800 metres of one of the stations of the north LRT line is a perfect transportation node. Studies of public transit riders find that 800 metres is the limit they consider convenient to have access to the station, so this would be a perfect transportation node

Apartment Buildings That Outperform

By focusing on apartment buildings near an LRT station, investors solve a transportation node within a single demographic. In this example of a niche, the investors' properties wouldn't necessarily be in close proximity, but they would be concentrated around a specific geographic feature (specific LRT stations). Whereas our previous example (condo-style rentals to near ring roads) targeted drivers, this niche targets LRT riders. It's a geographic niche that fits a completely different transportation node problem.

Niche Strategy – Geography

Not every blue-collar worker is also an LRT rider, which means not every blue-collar worker would be attracted to this sub-niche, and that's the point of being a niche-focused investor. Knowing that a target tenant-type wants to live near an LRT station lets the investor make better decisions about operations, marketing, branding and renovations. The entire process smoothens out.

Employment Nodes

Investors need to make a well-informed and strategic decision about whether or not a geographic niche is large enough. We will discuss this idea below. The professional rule of thumb is to clearly define one's niche down as small and specialized as possible for your investing goals. Expand your niche only when you must or when it hurts not to.

If the niche is large enough, but the pace of acquisitions would be too slow to reach your goals, then it's acceptable to identify a *secondary geographic niche* or slightly *expand your existing niche*.

Let's take a look at an example of a focused niche: In both Calgary and Edmonton there are several large hospitals that employ hundreds of nurses and technical workers. This is a large and significant employment node.

Realistically, this niche might be too small to fulfill acquisition goals. There may be less than one building within that niche that comes available every year (which is too small if purchasing a building per year is the goal). Basing acquisition rates realistically on a five offers to one successful acquisition ration, the nurses and technical workers niche may not be large enough to fulfill the reasonable and prudent goal of acquiring one building per year.

In such a case, the investor would need to open up a larger niche to achieve his or her goals every single year. Having a 'secondary niche' strategy is a good idea (with the caveat that you buy the building in the nurse niche whenever possible and you actively tilt the playing field in your favor so the odds of winning the next available building increase with each passing year). The patient investor uses secondary niches while slowly concentrating holdings, trading off other holdings for those within the niche through the disposition/reposition process.

The goal of future phases is to consolidate one's position. You've probably heard that it's wise strategy to 'sell your dogs' in a hot market, but what a makes a property a dog? A dog is just a property that doesn't fit an investor's niche. It's always that property in a portfolio that seems to cause all the trouble. Yes, there are some proto-typical dogs, but most often a dog is just a property that doesn't fit an investor's system.

Why would an investor bother purchasing a property that wasn't in his or her niche to begin with? It's not that investors intend to buy outside their niche; rather they learn more about their niche and define it better over time. Even the most strategic investors don't understand their geographic or demographic niche from the beginning. It takes in the trenches, practical knowledge to gain a complete understanding of the niche.

Niche Strategy – Geography

A great example of re-focusing within its niche is Boardwalk, which is a massive, publicly traded multi-family real estate company. Boardwalk (being a big company) has a big niche. They dominate the niche of multi-family towers near post-secondary institutions. This is where they got their start in, and they've made some excellent strategic decisions to take control of this niche over the past several years.

I consider Boardwalk a focused company, yet even they have purchased and disposed of several assets outside their niche over the past decade. This could mean they haven't always been as focused as they are now, or it could mean they simply chose a secondary niche, which they knew all along would be used as a tool to niche-up later.

Professionals (and in this case institutional investors) improve over time. It's one of the hallmarks of success. You're allowed to make mistakes, but you're not allowed to keep making the same mistakes for long. Successful investors learn where they are strong and consolidate within that niche.

Boardwalk is a high-end strategic success. On the opposite end of the spectrum was a young investor (I will call him Bill) that came and went (the rising (and falling) star syndrome) during the boom and bust cycle of the mid-2000s.

Bill made a lot of mistakes during his short tenure as a rising real estate star, the largest of which was a failure to niche. Bill's 'strategy' could be summarized in two words: buy Edmonton. For a couple of years this was exactly what he did. Bill was excellent at attracting investor money, but lacking a niche-focus he didn't excel at other aspects of investing.

Bill roped in a lot of investors with his infectious excitement and purchased about 100 units across Edmonton, mostly in small buildings – a mix of townhouses, duplexes, small multi-family, and pretty much everything that looked like a deal.

Bill's failure to focus and niche were emblematic of the amateur problem. Pros stand the test of time. They understand that indiscriminate action is no stand-in for strategy. The professional approach is scalable on the upside, and on the downside they make clearer, simpler decisions, rather than responding to a crisis or emotion.

Pros take strategic action rather than indiscriminate action. Bill was exposed, in the end, like so many naked swimmers when the tide went out (thanks for that one Warren Buffett). Bill's indiscriminate amateur action created a big mess.

When the difficult times came, not only was Bill over-leveraged, but his holdings were fanned out across the city in so many niches that they were impossible to optimize and manage – even if he did have the cash, which he didn't.

Without a legacy strategy, Bill was all about getting rich quick and was a firm believer in the vague and distant dream of, 'passive income'. As a result, Bill had a naïve approach to property management. He was completely hands-off; believing the property manager could solve any problem.

Experienced investors know that property management is important but that investors must oversee their managers in order to succeed.

The only way Bill's strategy would've worked is if the market continued to appreciate at 10 per cent annually, which appears to have been his 'strategy'. Unfortunately, there was a five-year period of falling or flat values, and he was wiped out by poor strategy and operations. He couldn't hang in there.

When Bill's primary lender backed out of the Canadian market, his portfolio was exposed. No other lender would take on the hodge-podge of underwater properties.

Bill started with goals but no legacy strategy. This infected his thinking in every business decision, including his inability to focus on a niche. The idea of limiting himself to a specific niche seemed like small thinking to him at the time.

Bill thought real estate would be glamorous, but in the end he got bogged down in the un-glamorous world of operational hell. He was stuck in a tenant quagmire, unable to replicate success across his hodge-podge portfolio. Imagine having to hustle for every new tenant rather than filling vacancies within a system. Imagine having to find a new crew for every renovation. Who was his ideal tenant? What renovations made sense for his tenant type? He didn't know, and as a result he didn't last long.

Bill 'followed the money' to Edmonton, thinking this was a niche. Unfortunately, if you can choose your niche by reading a general article in the business section of a daily newspaper it's not a niche.

There is a well-known business axiom that to thrive in business, one must solve a specific problem. This is the creation of value. Bill didn't solve anyone's particular problem, and a business that doesn't solve a problem doesn't remain a business for very long.

It may seem like I'm hammering on Bill, but in many ways he was just a victim of the time. Those were heady times when he entered the market. Bill was the proverbial case of the 'last one into the market' in a boom time. When everyone thought the party would never end, many people blindly believed in 'the power of a positive mindset'. It was believed that this could stand in for strategic thinking. It can't. Strategy is required.

Towards a Science of Niche Selection

We've spoken a lot about the importance of making a niche as small as practically possible, as focused as possible, and as rational as possible. This brings up the possibility of being over-niched. In such a case, the investor puts too much criterion around buying decisions and is stuck in analysis paralysis. This is a real threat, but there are far more active investors suffering Bill's problem, which was under-niching.

I'm assuming here that most investors stuck in analysis paralysis aren't there by over-niching but just by simple overthinking.

Niche Strategy – Geography

Nevertheless, over-niching is a risk and is worthwhile discussing. I know investors that confine their niche to a small set of 20 to 30 square blocks within a certain neighborhood. This may seem tiny, but as long as most properties are of a similar type, and available to the investors, then it could be large enough depending on the investor's goals. In a 30 square-block range, there will be a consistent churn of properties that come available for purchase, which could easily be a big enough niche.

Mainstreet Equities, another major Edmonton multi-family player seems to confine itself to such a geographic limitation, although as it is a major player, the size is larger than 30 blocks. Mainstreet focuses on a few neighbourhoods that have an abundance of similar buildings (multi-family buildings between 15 and 30 units). They buy aggressively within their niche, put it into their system, normalize it, optimize it, and reap the benefits of niche domination.

When I spoke earlier about servicing the nurse and tech trade demographics around large hospitals might be an example of a niche that is too small to fulfill the need for expansion, depending on the investor's expansion goals. If so, the investors would need a sub-niche to continue growing.

A backup niche can serve investors well – not only to ensure large enough niche but also to hedge against the overreliance on one small area if there are any major economic shifts. For example, if focused on nurse-residence style buildings and there is a significant government cutback for hospitals, then having a backup niche that's not dependent upon the nurse niche will help hedge against losing the nurse niche.

So, how can a focused investor be certain their niche is the correct size? Furthermore, how does an investor develop a plan worthy of her goals? How does she tilt the playing field in favor of achieving her goals? There are three tasks an investor must undertake to select, enter, and dominate a niche:

1. **Create Goals**: The investor must start by considering her legacy strategy. From this, the investor can create goals. Notice it's not the other way around, as Bill believed. Legacy strategy comes before goals.

    Goals are necessary for niche selection, since the first step of selecting a Goldilocks niche (not to big, not too small, and just right) is to know how many properties you want to own and in what time frame. It's wise to set goals in five year increments. This is a long enough period for planning a coherent strategy, yet it's short enough to recognize the fact that goals change over time.

2. **Define and Track Acquisition Activity Metrics**: Once goals are set, the investor must calculate which activity (and how much) will lead to the desired result. This is no different than the old-fashioned sales-training standard, where you develop and follow metrics for effort, not results.

    Anyone that has ever done sales knows that success boils down to activity (so long as it's the correct activity). You can't control the market or anyone else's behavior, but you can control effort and activity. After selecting goals, you must then set activity standards that will ensure meeting the goals.

The most important activity metric in real estate is *writing offers*. Meeting offer writing targets will ensure you meet acquisition targets.

The next metrics to track are whatever activities it takes to uncover acquisition targets. In other words, in order to find the properties to write offers on, you first need to do certain activities to find properties to offer on.

An example of such an activity might be to look at 50 properties online every week, or maybe you physically visit five properties every week.

3. **Research Niche Size:**- Once you've created goals, activities, and activity metrics, the next step is to identify whether or not there are enough properties in the niche.

   This will involve you researching exactly how many buildings are located in your target niche. It's like looking at a catalogue of buildings you will purchase one day. If a building isn't available, then you just think of it as being out of stock. So, you simply wait until it comes back into stock.

   Knowledge is power. By knowing the buildings in advance you can radically tilt the playing field.

By following the above three steps investors can ensure they've selected a large enough niche. If, at the end of these three steps, you discover that your niche is too small, you then expand your niche. Later, when the opportunity arises you reposition to further cement yourself in your niche.

Tight-Niching, Tilting the Playing Field, Opportunism

Perry (not his real name) is a multi-family investor in Edmonton with a strong focus on the working class west-end neighbourhoods. What's outstanding about Perry is his dual-track of action taking. He's both niche focused and opportunistic at the same time.

If a multi-family building comes available within Perry's niche, he will make an offer – no exceptions. If he finds out that you own a building in an area he'd like to buy, you can expect phone calls once a month until you're dead. He never misses a chance to write an offer in his niche, and everyone connected with real estate in the city knows this. In other words, Perry has tilted the playing field in his favor.

Perry is so good at tilting the playing field that more than half of the commercial real estate professionals in Edmonton will call Perry first if a property in his niche comes available. When they call, chances are that Perry already knows as much about the building as they do.

Do you think Perry has enough opportunities to buy in his niche? How would you like to have half of all agents working for you?

Niche Strategy – GEOGRAPHY

Tilting the playing field in this way takes time and effort, but the effort is well worth it.

Perry's story illustrates how niche ownership opens up possibilities. Pros like Perry know this. Amateurs think the opposite – that niching down limits possibilities. By putting geographic (and other) restrictions on what you'll buy, you actually allow yourself to find and buy more excellent properties, not fewer.

However, Perry has an exception to his niche focus. He will buy a good deal if one comes across his desk even if it's not in his wheelhouse – so long as he can understand it's position in the value chain and the property's lifespan. This doesn't mean Perry chases every deal he sees.

If a great deal shows op that can be managed within his existing portfolio, then he will write up an offer, sometimes within hours of seeing the property. Don't make the mistake of thinking Perry is unfocused, though. He is hyper-focused, but he's aware that it's okay to opportunistically buy outside his niche and then use the asset to reposition later (much more on this later).

Perry figured out his activity metrics a long time ago and consistently stuck to them. Over the years, Perry has carefully built a reputation as a serious buyer. It's taken him years but he's now reaping the rewards.

CHAPTER 4
Niche Strategy – Demographics

"You've Got Mail"

AOL

Specialization Equals Results

People born around 1982 (my era) are much different than those born in 1996. My cohorts and I looked forward to turning 16-years old so I could get my driver's license. I had my driver's test booked as close as humanly possible to the day I turned 16. I couldn't wait to drive my 1986 Nissan King Cab pickup that my friends and I lovingly called 'mini-keg'. Driving represented freedom, our highest value.

My friends and I saved up our summer job incomes, bought rickety old cars, and hit the road with pride. We didn't care much about style or comfort. We didn't find it embarrassing to drive a crappy car. We simply loved the freedom.

Apartment Buildings That Outperform

Today's young people, between 16 and 25, don't care in the same numbers that we did back in the 'old days'.

I can't say why for certain, but it's simply not as high of priority value to today's 16-25 year olds. Perhaps it's caused by fuel prices, fear of the dangers of driving, or perhaps the urban culture of cafes and walk-able streets is more ingrained in the youth. Perhaps they just have fewer reasons to leave home, preferring to interact with friends via social media and play video games rather than seek thrills on the open road. Maybe it's because they've grown up in the global warming generation. Perhaps their parents sheltered them more – whereas my generation and those previous would spend all of our waking hours playing on the street with the neighbourhood kids, today's young adults are the first generation of inside kids.[4]

I don't totally understand it, and I don't need to in this context. As an investor you don't need to know all of the reasons, either. You simply have to know that less young people driving is a demographic trend not likely to go away soon.

This is an example of a classic demographic shift. Something changed amongst the millennial kids that have made fewer of them want to drive. We don't need to understand it, but we need to adjust to it.

---

4 For a great discussion about the indoor generation and the idea of nature deficit disorder read Richard Louv's 2005 book *Last Child in the Woods*.

Niche Strategy – Demographics

What does this mean for multi-family investors? It might mean everything, or it might mean nothing. Not every investor will target the millennial generation, but every investor needs a target demographic.

Investors don't need to understand the root causes of the demographic trends, but they need to understand the trends themselves. Not knowing can be very dangerous. Out of touch investors aren't well informed enough to make effective decisions.

This trend of fewer young drivers was brought home to me a few months ago when I was showing a small multi-family building to a renovation-focused investor. The building was partway through a major renovation when the previous owner ran out of money and steam. He was selling to escape, and the property was perfect for my opportunistic renovation buyer.

The building was in the 124th street district of Edmonton, an area undergoing rapid transition. All of the various factors have coalesced, so the street and its surrounding area have officially taken off as a hotspot of cool in the city of Edmonton, with trendy food trucks everywhere and a cool farmer's market.

It's not dissimilar to the Whyte Avenue area's transition (across the river) about 20-25 years ago. For those readers not familiar with Edmonton, think 17th Ave. in Calgary, Gastown in Vancouver, or the Beaches in Toronto.

As usual, the first ones to the area are the youngest and hippest – the trendsetters. This means the millennial kids and renters. The area is becoming a haven for cool young renters – the trendsetters for the next two decades.

It was doubly interesting that day as we walked through the property because the client brought his 25-year old daughter with him. His plan was for his daughter to live in the building as she was about to begin studying at Grant McEwan University, which is only a few blocks away from the property. She was there to approve whether she wanted to live in the building or not, but she ended up providing us with an investment insight.

The investor, whose plan was to finish the renovation before renting all 10 units, was doing his diligence and therefore asking good questions. Eventually, he asked about parking for the building, which is often an important factor.

This was already on my mind, as the property had only the minimum legal number of parking spaces. It was a critical strike against the property, and I knew it. I told the buyer how many parking spaces were available and pointed out it was a bit low. As suspected, he was concerned about this problem.

This investor knew his stuff. He knew that having few parking spots is usually a big problem. He began hinting that the lack of parking might be a deal breaker. Sensing that he was on the edge, I played a hunch.

I turned to the daughter and said, "Tell me, do you drive?"

"Umm, no actually," she said.

"What about your friends?" I said.

"Nobody drives nowadays," she said.

"Care to explain?" said her father.

"Fewer than half of my friends have a driver's license. Of those that have a license, only about half have a car," she said.

My hunch turned out to be correct, and her father's facial expression changed from concern to amusement, "as long as the building is full of people like her, then I guess there is plenty of parking," he said.

This led to a discussion of the area, how it was transitioning fast, and how the millennial generation doesn't drive. Without me saying it directly, the investor came to the conclusion that the building was perfect for the millennial generation, which he knew would be the target niche.

Many of the millennial kids don't even have cars, let alone trailers, second cars, or boats. If anything they have scooters and bicycles, neither of which requires a parking space.

After discussing for a few minutes, the investor even began musing that perhaps he could rent the extra parking stalls out for a tidy additional profit. I assured him that this was possible, since the building was close to a busy commercial area.

The parking was actually abundant in this building, and its excess may prove to be a valuable asset to the investors. The investor's daughter opened the door, and we received further confirmation about the power of a demographic from her words. It still remains to be seen how that'll change when they have kids and form families.

By choosing the right demographic in the right geographic location, investors can leverage time, resources, and energy to achieve maximum results. Assets perform better when the investor understands the demographic, since he can take focused and decisive action across the spectrum of acquisition, optimization, and disposition

Demographics and Cohorts

Demographics is the study of statistical data about a group. Cohorts are groups of people with shared cultural experience of a time.

Within cohorts there are demographic trends. My cohort shares the demographic trend of 'many drivers'. The cohort of current 19-25 year olds shares the demographic trend of 'fewer drivers'.

We can narrow down the classifications of people (and tenant types) by shared factors. Let's look at a list of attributes of my client's ideal tenant type:

- Between 19 and 25 years old
- Doesn't drive
- Attending downtown university (Grant McEwan or NAIT)
- Non-smoker
- Rides a bike or scooter
- Comfortable navigating transit

Niche Strategy – Demographics

When you put all of these attributes together, you have a specific demographic for the purposes of marketing. In this way, the investor has identified his ideal tenant type.

The first thing we know about them is that they are members of the millennial cohort, but by identifying the demographic trends of many within that cohort, he has come up with his true demographic (ideal tenant type).

This is a vital distinction to make when choosing a niche. Remember, a niche is geographic, but it's moreover a type of person that engages in a type of behaviour.

Demographic trends are when a statistically significant subset of the population behaves in a certain way. Sometimes that trend is limited to within a single cohort, and other times the behavior is spread across several cohorts.

Today's millennial kids have taken to Snapchat, but very few baby boomers are on Snapchat. On the other hand, baby boomers are on Facebook in huge numbers. It stands to reason, then, that Facebook is a better place to reach baby boomers than Snapchat.

With demographic trends come opportunities. We're all aware of the baby boomer cohort, as whole industries have risen up in each distinct phase of baby boomers' lives to service their changing needs.

For example, the minivan era began when baby boomers started having kids. This demographic trend within the cohort saved the Chrysler Corporation and started a sub-category of product by solving a major problem.

As the baby boomers got older, Viagra was born. And as they age even further, the adult diaper industry will flourish. This is already happening in Japan, where the population is older than North America.

Adult diapers *outsell* baby diapers in Japan. The Japanese population is aging, and as a result there is a growing demographic trend of 'adult diaper wearers'. Businesses in Japan will cash in on that trend in more sectors than just the adult diaper industry, too.

Demographic trends drive the economy, including real estate. This is why we follow trends and ignore fads.

Potentially Marginal Demographic Niches (fads not trends)

If the niche you're targeting is likely to pull up stakes and leave, it may be a risky niche. The short-term results might be stellar, but such instability won't allow you to build a real estate investing business. If tenants are likely to leave it means their behaviour is a fad, not a trend. This phenomenon happens on both ends of the spectrum – from high-end to low-end.

A couple of months ago, I spoke with a young and prosperous millennial couple (let's call them John and Sally). They told me an interesting story about their housing situation. Their example is informative to any investors seeking to understand the sometimes-inexplicable behaviour of a demographic.

Niche Strategy – Demographics

John and Sally had been renting a high-end condo-style property in an upscale neighborhood of St. Albert (an already upscale suburb of the Edmonton region). When I spoke with them they'd been living in this property for a year.

The building looks fabulous. It's new, has high-end features, and is targeted towards young millennials with money like John and Sally. These young people are accustomed to living well, and when they move out of their parents' home they want to move into a high-end property, whether renting or buying.

John is a safety inspector and Sally is an office manager. Together, they had a great income. For the owner of the building this was an accidental niching success. John and Sally found the building because friends of theirs (same demographic) told them about it. The owner charged significant rents, as one would expect for a high-end rental product.

It sounds like a perfect strategy for the investor, but in-fact this can be a tough niche to capture. The reason is simple: if your target tenant can afford to spend so much on renting it means they can also qualify for a mortgage.

They are renters by choice rather than necessity. This makes them fickle. To keep them for long, the investor has to make the renting experience excellent or else they will simply buy a home because they have options.

Unfortunately for the investor, John and Sally's renting experience wasn't excellent. There were problems with the building – air conditioning, foundation settlement, wall cracking. Remember that John and Sally's cohort is highly active across all social media platforms. They told me that the problems with their building were so well known amongst their social group that there was even a hashtag for it. The building's problems were shared on social media hundreds of times.

John and Sally decided, after only a few months of renting, that they didn't like renting and that it was time to move into a home of their own. They went to the bank and found out that they qualified for a $500,000 mortgage. They started looking for a home immediately.

For the investor, the fickleness of the niche might not be such a big problem if it's still supported by a demographic trend of people flowing towards the niche (as it is in this case). Still, if your niche can pull up stakes at any moment you will constantly be dealing with tenant turnover. To counteract this problem, branding and marketing must continue to attract a flow of new tenants.

There are more fickle examples, too.

For example, I know of an investor whose niche was super-suited furnished homes around West Edmonton Mall. A super-suite is just a house or apartment that rents by the room. In some super-suites, the tenants even share a bedroom.

This investor rented two-bedroom apartments to four people that each paid him $500 per month. $2000 per month for a two-bedroom apartment is incredible in

Edmonton. Traditional rent for the same apartment would earn him about $1150 per month.

Some investors love this and have tried to make a niche out of it. This raises the question: which demographic does this serve? What is the niche that these investors are targeting?

In Alberta, this type of living situation is rare. Only some students and temporary foreign workers are usually willing to share an apartment with people they don't know. Even these two demographics prefer (and will switch) to live with people they know.

Typically, landlords want to see a bit of a job history and rental history, so the super-suited places actually served a useful function in helping renters move from temporary accommodations into a more permanent home. After a few months in a super-suite, a tenant can get a more permanent dwelling, as they develop a tenancy history.

The tenant turnover in super-suited homes is consistent, and investors doing super-suites knew this. To them it was worth it because of the higher rental incomes. They knew there would be turnover, but they assumed there would be a consistent supply of new renters.

However, as of the time of this writing, the temporary foreign worker program in Alberta has been shut down due to public anger caused by poor communication by the government (and abuse of the program by a few employers).

The investors that focused on this niche must now do what they can to make their properties work without temporary foreign workers (switching to the student niche for example), sell, or wait for the program to open up again. The investor I mentioned doesn't have the luxury of switching to the student niche, as his properties are nowhere near a university or a college.

The temporary foreign worker niche dried up overnight. Basing his business on super-suited temporary foreign worker niche seemed like great wisdom at the time, but now it appears these investors mistook a fad for a trend.

Marginal demographics tend to breed problems. Focus on the big demographic trends and carve out a specialty within it.

Stable Demographic Niches (Trends not Fads)

To select a stable and successful niche, focus on stable demographic trends. By understanding the larger forces of population shifts and economics, you will be able to better understand what makes a demographic trend stable or not. Let's take a look at some stable demographic trends to build a niche on.

Immigrant Service Sector Workers

Above, we discussed how the temporary foreign worker niche was unstable. However, the demographic trend of new immigrants working in the service sector is very stable in Alberta. Whereas the temporary foreign worker program was easy to abolish (and it will likely be easy to bring back), the trend of (permanent) immigrants is here to stay.

We know it's stable because of the overall Alberta economy, which is growing rapidly and is predicted to continue growing. The Alberta job market has been notoriously tight for most of the 21st century. Most workers are absorbed by the high-paying oil industry. As a result, the service sector has to look overseas to fill positions. Visit any service-related business in most of Alberta, and you will quickly notice that new Canadians fill most of the positions.

These new Canadians typically rent for the first few years as they get established in Canada. Around a major retail area, like Chinook Mall in Calgary for example, the two-bedroom suite rental market will be strong for a long time to come due to this stable demographic shift based on a real economic need.

Blue-Collar Lifetime Renters

In Edmonton, there is a strong long-term demographic trend of blue-collar workers. These folks are small-engine mechanics, CNC operators, heavy equipment operators, and truck drivers. They may be baby boomers, Gen-X, millennial or immigrants.

There are some major advantages of targeting this niche, even though many hate the idea. The types of properties blue-collar workers live in tend to be run-down and a bit gritty. This turns many buyers off, but I personally love this niche.

Another Edmonton realtor and I were recently discussing a property she was selling in this niche the other day. She told me she was dealing with a perception problem on this property. Buyers were happy to walkthrough the 17-suite building but were immediately turned off by the smell of smoke since smokers occupied 14 of the 17 units.

I'm a non-smoker, and like most non-smokers, I find the smell of smoke disgusting, but as an investor, I recognize that there is opportunity in renting to smokers. As a group, smokers have been pushed to the margins of society. Our society has become very judgmental, and there are very few places smokers can smoke in peace.

Smokers are Great Renters

In my years in the residential real estate business, I've come to realize that smokers can be awesome renters. This is true for a single reason: once in a building they never leave.

There are so few options available to smokers that they end up staying in an apartment when they get one. The pain of trying to find a new apartment that will let them smoke is enough to keep them where they are.

If you have an apartment building full of smokers (and small dog owners), you will deal with fewer tenant turnovers than most landlords.

When I investigated the 17-suite building's history, I found my prediction to be accurate. The building had an unbelievably low turnover for the past 10 years. Most of the units hadn't turned over for at least five years.

Of course, there are negatives to owning a smoking building. For example, you will have to replace the furnace more often if there is one. In addition, you will have a hard time remediating the smell and stains on the wall if you ever want to turn the building into a non-smoking building.

You will have a harder time selling the building for as much as you would if the building was non-smoking. This means you must purchase it for less to make up for the lower sale price with better margins.

Still, if you can show a several year history of higher rents and stable tenancy, then you should be able to offset much of the lower sale price. Charging higher rent is easily justified, as everyone, including smokers, is aware of the damage to property caused by smoking. You simply charge more for the damage smoking will undoubtedly cause.

One helpful tool for dealing with the smell of smoke in a building is to use something called a 'make up air unit'. Essentially, this is a forced air heater used in conjunction with radiant hot water heaters (from a boiler unit). When used in conjunction the radiant heaters will heat each individual suite, but the make up air unit will force air into the common areas.

> These are not usually necessary for heating, which is why many of them never get repaired after they break down, but they serve a vital function in keeping smells from exiting individual suites. Make up air unit keeps air pressure in the common areas higher than in suites, thereby forcing air *into* suites rather than letting air (and the smells that come along with it) into the hallway.
>
> Make up air units aren't the perfect antidote for the smell of smoke, but using one might be the only effective way to run a mixed smoker/non-smoker building.

This blue-collar niche, which crosses several cohorts and demographics, is a great example of a stable niche. There are plenty of blue-collar jobs in Edmonton, and the economic trends of the future promise many thousands more will be created. You can speak directly to this niche in your branding and marketing efforts, and you can build a solid business on this niche.

Students

Sprinkled throughout Canada, there are several cities with higher than average student populations. Edmonton is one such city. We have NAIT, Grant McEwan, the University of Alberta, and several smaller institutions of higher learning. The student population here is a major advantage to Edmonton's economy, as it balances the instability of our resource based economy.

Some niche focused investors even niche-down to subgroups of students. As mentioned previously, some investors cater to the trade schools of NAIT and other tiny sub-niches.

There are some downsides to renting to students. Namely, they tend to be slobs that love partying and they move nearly every year. Turnover is high.

Still, focused landlords make the student niche work by bulletproofing operations. They only rent to students with a parent's co-signature on the lease, and they charge above average rents by super-suiting.

Millennial Hipsters

This is a large subset of the millennial demographic. They are digital natives. They are knowledge workers, and they place a high value on the cool factor, without caring much for many of the same things their parents did, such as owning a home. As mentioned above, they don't even care much for cars.

Members of this demographic are ideal renters, as they plan on renting for a long time, which makes them a stable, long-term demographic niche. These "hipsters" are huge in number. They (like their baby boomer parents) make up 27 per cent of the population. They are the natural inheritors of the future due to their size.

Money Millennials

This group is in the same cohort with the 'hipster' millennials, but they have different values (at least during the years between 19 and 25.

Apartment Buildings That Outperform

Rather than spending a long time in school or otherwise waiting for income, they have joined the workforce and started making money right away – a special privilege of Alberta young adults over other provinces due to the remarkable Alberta job market.

This group has never lacked for anything, and their tastes reflect this. They like nice homes, whether renting or buying, and they are discernible by their taste for brands. Remember John and Sally mentioned above? John drives a $50,000 pickup truck and Sally a $75,000 SUV.

As renters, they can be fickle, since they have the choice to buy. Renting is a lifestyle choice for them, so you must be aware of this if you try to capture this niche.

The main difference between them and their hipster brethren is that they drive. This makes their behaviour distinctive, and as such they tend to prefer the suburbs to high-density downtown living. If they do live in a condo it will be a high-end one preferably with underground parking.

CHAPTER 5

The Value Chain Strategy – Optimization

"Buy, Fix, Sell. Repeat."

Chris Davies

A Strategic Success Story

Recently, a client shared a success story with me. I wanted to share it here because it's a perfect example of the strategic professional investor's approach. Peter (not his real name) is relatively new to the multi-family arena, and although he has had a few hiccups along the way, he has grasped the professional mindset quickly.

Peter's first few apartment building purchases were successful, but it wasn't until his third that he got it right. His first two buildings were steady earners, but the third was a true strategic success.

He became aware of all the factors that make a deal strategically successful, and he executed on the strategy.

This is no small feat. It's one thing to understand what would make a deal successful, but it's another to execute strategically.

So, what did Peter do?

He applied specific strategies we discuss in this book. He paid attention to geography, demographics, financing strategy, and especially optimization.

In his acquisition phase, Peter had his eye on the *overall strategy,* which is the true hallmark of a professional investor. This means he didn't buy for the sake of buying. Instead he selected a property that was perfect for a strategic treatment throughout all the three main stages of the investing process: acquisition, optimization and disposition.

First, Peter had learned to purchase properties based on the economic fundamentals (macro geography), but he also purchased on the micro geography (his specific corner of Edmonton). This allowed him to bring on an onsite manager who was already managing a building nearby.

Next, Peter capitalized on a demographic niche (his specialty), which allowed him to raise rents an average of $50 higher per door above comparable suites. He carefully targeted a demographic, and then tailored operations and branding for that demographic. This helped maximize tenant retention and referrals.

Peter also capitalized on clever financing. He purchased with little cash and secured excellent long-term financing on the property. His monthly payments were extremely low, which improved his (already stellar) cash flow.

Finally, and by far most important to his story, Peter employed strategic renovations to raise the value (after renovation expenses were paid) by over $100,000 and cash flow by over $1,000 per month. How was this possible?

He identified a 15-unit apartment building that had been undermanaged for years, and as a result had not been optimized for maximum cash flow and value. In addition to some small focused renovations to the common areas and for external curb appeal, Peter recognized on this initial walkthrough that the he could convert four of the seven bachelor suites into one-bedroom suites. He also recognized that the laundry room was too big and by carving up some of the laundry room space he could combine it with another bachelor suite to add a fifth one-bedroom suite.

This radical change in the suite mix raised the rents (and therefore the value) dramatically, and the entire renovation was carried out with minimal impact on building vacancies. This was partially the result of excellent operations, as Peter's management team was perfectly situated to execute the renovation.

Peter did this for under $50,000 in renovation expenses, and since he doesn't live in Edmonton, he rarely even visited the property site during construction.

In other words, from start to finish, Peter carried out the project with professional level strategy and execution. It was the type of result that builds business and *enables legacy*. The truth is that Peter is an aggressive investor, and he will buy several more buildings over the course of his investing career, but if he were to so choose, he wouldn't need much more than this single building to secure his legacy as a great Edmonton investor and realize a brighter future for those important to him.

Every investor can replicate Peter's success by following the same steps.

Investors without a value-chain strategy muddle along, bemoaning the ongoing and never-ending renovation expenses of the business. Professional investors expect, and indeed find opportunity, in the very same renovations. They know optimization is the path up the value chain.

However, renovations are just one component of the optimization phase. Even if a property wasn't purchased strategically, investors still exert enormous control of the result through consistent optimization, but when strategic buying goes hand in hand with well-executed optimization the results are stellar (as with Peter).

This is the professional investor's job. Many think real estate is a "buy it and forget it game," but it isn't. How well an investor optimizes is the difference between professionalism and amateurism.

Remember, even a pro can make a mistake on the purchase, but a true pro will find a way to battle through the bad early start and win. Just as a championship team has to fight through deficits during a playoff run, so does a pro investor fight through a few poor purchases.

Rule: Where we can optimize, we must optimize.

This is the professional multi-family investor's mantra. Ignore it at your peril.

The Value Chain Strategy – Optimization

Remember the story of Diane we spoke of above? Dispersing her holdings far and wide ended up being a strategic mistake, but she didn't just quit. She optimized her way out of trouble.

She optimized through the struggle of trying to find excellent property managers in strange lands. She optimized through the crippling problem of bad mortgages and crumbling rental markets. She optimized and optimized even when things looked bleak and when she was overextended almost to the point where the situation looked hopeless and a lesser investor would have packed it in.

In the process, she survived some tricky situations and came out as a stronger investor. Furthermore, her portfolio and team came out the other side lean and mean. In geology, pressure makes diamonds. In real estate, pressure helps investors raise their game.

But let's assume for a moment, that, unlike Diane, you don't make a buying mistake. In such a case, rather than optimizing for survival, you'll be optimizing for maximum effect – for value creation and cash flow growth. You'll be optimizing as part of a plan already concocted when you purchased the property and the portfolio as a whole.

This is the beautiful coming together of the professional elements, and is the perfect scenario. This is strategy on a high level, and this is what multi-family investors must seek out.

I've just described a perfect scenario – a theory. In reality, every investor I know spends part of his or her time optimizing haphazardly purchased properties and part of his or her time optimizing well planned and thought out properties. The really smart ones 'dump their dogs' and use the capital from the sale to go deeper into their niche.

A great example of optimization is Mainstreet Equities – one of Edmonton's larger multi-family players. If you've ever seen one of their buildings, it means you've seen them all. Mainstreet is systematized to the point of boring while still keeping its scrappy street cred. They also optimize with such boring efficiency that it brings a (happy) tear to my eye.

So, how do they do it?

First, they buy strategically. In its public filings, Mainstreet has identified a hyper-specific target region. It is currently pursuing an aggressive growth strategy around the Edmonton Municipal Airport, which is closing down and being converted to mixed commercial and residential usage. I think that Mainstreet is only at the beginning of this play.

Mainstreet is even liquidating some Ontario and British Columbia assets to focus its efforts on acquiring in their tiny target area around the airport. However, many of Mainstreet's existing properties are in other neighbourhoods not far from the Municipal Airport district –Oliver, Queen Mary Park, Central McDougall, Prince Charles and Inglewood.

Mainstreet is replicating the template from its established niche neighbourhoods with the new play (Municipal Airport). These micro-regions provide them an optimization dream scenario.

Especially when it comes to marketing and advertising, Mainstreet reaps massive benefit from niching. Its domination of the Oliver district online ad space is total. If you wanted to rent in Oliver, it would be nearly impossible to avoid considering Mainstreet as one of your first choices.

The sheer number of units Mainstreet owns makes its advertising blitz all the more powerful, but smaller investors can produce a similar result on a smaller scale through consistency, database marketing, and branding. This is marketing optimization at its finest, a component of value-chain strategy for multi-family investors.

This chapter will include a detailed discussion of the various ways that professional multi-family investors optimize their assets.

We're All Value-Chain Investors

The Mainstreet example of efficiently moving up the value-chain is very instructive to individual investors, since individual investors are almost all forced by necessity to invest in this way.

This value-chain strategy is all about creating wealth, which is a much different goal than preserving wealth. Wealth preservation is a common mode of operation for some of the biggest multi-family players in the market but not necessarily with Mainstreet. They're focused on wealth creation.

Wealth preservation firms purchase buildings that have less potential for value creation but also will have less need for future capital investment. Whereas a company like Mainstreet may seek to drive up the value of its stock through aggressive acquisition and value-creation strategies, the wealth preservation companies focus on cash flow and funds from operations. Their investors sit on their stock forever to collect dividends and preserve wealth. Growth is considered a bonus for these firms. Due to this strategy, wealth preservation firms often attract pension fund money and other large chunks of conservative cash.

Most individual investors don't have the luxury of such a strategy. Sure, there is the odd investor who has inherited family money or is redirecting a windfall from a previous business (or lottery winnings) into real estate. For the most part individual investors are seeking to use real estate as a wealth creation vehicle more than (only) a wealth preservation tool.

Moving up the value-chain is a lynchpin of successful real estate investing for most of us. Both types of investors (wealth creation and wealth preservation) profit over the long term by riding markets, but the value-chain investor forces value growth by excellent execution.

CHAPTER 6

Value Chain Strategy – Valuation and Financing

> *"Price is what you pay. Value is what you get."*
>
> **Warren Buffett**

Robert's Closet

Robert, a successful Edmonton investor, recently shared a (financing and valuation) success story with me that I think demonstrates the value chain strategy and how value can be created using only creativity, knowledge, and some hustle.

Do you want $109,000 for free?

You don't need to answer that. I know what you're going to say.

Robert liked the idea, too. In truth, it wasn't totally free. He had to do a few hours' work, file a few papers, and pay an administrative fee in order to get his $109,000. He even worked over the holidays.

Shocking, isn't it?

Then again, real estate investors sometimes work odd hours. Robert is a real pro, and he really did 'find' $109,000 of value in a property just by being creative, working hard, and doing a bit of marketing.

The property in question was a 10-suite apartment building that Robert had just purchased with a combination of cash and private money. His original plan was to do some renovations on the property and then get a long term, CMHC insured mortgage once renovations were complete – a standard and battle-tested strategy.

Robert already got an appraisal from the bank, which had assured him it would provide financing at a valuation of $109,000 per unit, for a total valuation of $1,090,000. With this time-tested successful strategy in place Robert judged that he would be happy with the property no matter what else happened. It was a good property that would cash flow nicely on a long-term hold.

If we ended the story right there Robert would have been happy with the outcome. It was a solid single. The kind every successful real estate investor builds a business on, but every pro wants to hit a homerun if possible.

Looking for that homerun, Robert asked the bank how much they'd lend him if he got a development permit for an existing cubbyhole-sized caretaker suite that was in the building. The bank said they'd provide a loan based on a

$1,199,000 valuation (109,000 x 11) if the nonconforming caretaker suite was made legal. In other words, they would value his new (small) unit equal with the others.

Robert asked the bank to put it in writing, which they did, and he went off in search of legal-suite status.

When he purchased the building, the suite was illegal. There was no permit for it, and Robert expected it would be a tough sell with the bank because the suite didn't have a bathroom. His only weapons in this fight were a hunch and some determination.

The lack of in-suite bathroom was a major strike against his case. However, there was a bathroom across the hallway that was accessible by walking through the laundry room. Robert wondered if he could use the bathroom across the hall as the suite's bathroom.

He dug in during the Christmas holiday and put together a 15-page package that included drawings, emergency egress routes, aerial photos, parking lot turning radius calculations, charts and more. In other words, he put in a professional effort.

Most importantly, he made it look professional by putting a professional cover on the application. This is the number one rule when dealing with the city: make it look good. In doing so, the chance of winning the development battle goes up exponentially. Robert put in a real effort and it looked great, but in truth it didn't take more than a couple of days' work.

Was it worth $109,000?

To his delight the permit application was accepted. Let's review how his pro maneuver played out.

First, Robert knew there was a potential asset in this tiny studio apartment. As we'll discuss later, the long (and smart) financing strategy is to put cheap CMHC money on your multi-family properties while holding for the long term. It's a great strategy but is only possible with the right property.

CMHC will lend only when the property is sufficiently renovated and well managed. The property in question needed renovations before Robert would qualify for cheap (sub 3 per cent interest rate) CMHC money. Renovating was his plan all along.

By presenting this initial plan to the bank he'd already secured the $1,090,000 valuation on the property. He was already in the process of adding value through renovations when he discovered the hidden gem of the property – an extra suite. Discovered might not be the word. He knew it was there when he bought it. Rather, he started thinking about ways to legalize the suite and therefore get financing for it.

Robert bought a 10-suite building, but he wanted to get financing on an 11-suiter. Not only did the sellers fail to manage and renovate the property well, they also failed to sell the building with as many units as were possible. In the end, the seller left a lot of value to be plucked up by Robert.

Pros naturally gravitate to the deals that amateurs sell, and this is right. The property was a solid single as he bought it, but it became a homerun with a bit of work and creativity.

Pros embrace creativity in every aspect of their game, but there are real opportunities for creativity in finance and valuation. Robert didn't act like a passive player in the valuation of his building, and neither should you. Creativity in financing and valuation is one of the most powerful components of the value-chain strategy. Knowing how and doing it well can mean all the difference between a single and a homerun.

Amateurs tend to think of real estate as 'passive'. They maintain fantasies about passive income, assuming that if they 'just rent it out' then money will fly through their open window. They believe that by purchasing in the right area they will win, but in reality picking an investing town or property type is less important than management and other optimization activities.

Pros know there is no such thing as passive income. They know they can reduce the onsite effort through systemization, but they never believe in the passive income fantasy. They work hard and apply active creativity to all aspects of the business – including valuation and financing.

Improving Valuation

Forcing up the value of holdings is a major key to success in multi-family investing. Failing to do so means underselling when many years later. In effect, investors that don't force valuation give up hundreds of thousands or millions of dollars because they aren't willing to do a bit of work.

If leaving money on the table in this way seems foreign and ridiculous to you then congratulations, but keep in mind it happens to most investors by accident. They don't foresee themselves getting lazy over the years. They start pinching pennies and only see expenses without understanding future value of improvements.

Stay hungry and stay active.

It's a shame when investors lose their gusto because there are several excellent strategies for moving up the value-chain. The investor's job is to identify such opportunities when they buy, and then capitalize on them when they own the property.

Let's walk step-by-step through several of these various methods of raising value.

Adding Suites

As we saw in Robert's (and Peter's) story, adding suites is a wonderful way to add value to a building. Multi-family buildings are valued on their income, which means if you can add one suite that will add $12,000 Net Operating Income (NOI) to the building, you are in effect adding $200,000 to the building's value, assuming a 6 per cent capitalization rate (cap rate).

> ### Calculating Cap Rate
>
> "The cap rate is the ratio of NOI to property asset value. For example, if a property was listed for one million and generated an NOI of $100,000, then the cap rate would be $100,000/one million, or 10 per cent."

The basic cap rate formula is:

cap rate = annual NOI/value (cost)

By calculating in this direction we use the property numbers (NOI and value) to figure out the cap rate. Note that the cap rate is what the return would be on the property if it were purchased for all cash.

However, the cap rate is more commonly used in the other direction. In this scenario we use the cap rate calculation like a tool to estimate what the value of the property would be based on a percentage of the NOI. In this case, we're not looking for the cap rate. Rather, we provide a cap rate as a means to value the property.

In this case the calculation looks like this:

value = NOI/cap Rate

With numbers:

$1,000,000 = $100,000/10 per cent

There are two things to note about using cap rate for valuations.

1. A proposed cap rate is merely a suggestion. Buyers and sellers will always have different idea of what the cap rate should be for valuation

2. The seller will never give perfectly accurate NOI numbers. The seller's goal is to sell for as much as possible, so they will always try to tilt the NOI numbers higher. It's the buyer's job to do all of the diligence necessary to get (truly) accurate NOI numbers.

Adding suites is a no-brainer – a tried and true way to add value. The only trouble is that not every building is a candidate for adding suites. This brings up the question: which buildings are candidates for adding suites?

Here are three ways to add suites to a property:

You can *add an additional floor* to an existing building. This strategy is more popular in some locations than others. In Canada, it's more common in Ontario than the West. In the past, Edmonton's extra geographical space has allowed builders to build further and further from the center of the city. However, we're currently coming into a time of great densification in housing, and as we will see the 'adding levels strategy' used more often.

To plan for and capitalize on this strategy, simply be aware of the zoning and building allowances. If you can execute the strategy early in the ownership and if it makes financial sense, then by all means go ahead and do it immediately. Otherwise, wait and add another level when finances make sense. Assuming there is 'normal' market appreciation, this should happen within a decade.

A second way to add suites is to *build additional buildings on the same property*. This strategy is an absolute homerun if you can do it. Here you are limited by the property's size and zoning restrictions. If you can execute this strategy, it could mean a multi-million dollar difference in wealth down the road.

Finally, you can *analyze the building and add suites wherever possible*. In past times architects and builders were less focused on maximizing the use of space in multi-family buildings. When looking around at older properties,

I'm always shocked by the irregularities. Many buildings have dead space just waiting to be used creatively.

Can you cut down the boiler room to half its size and add a suite (or even just a bedroom)? Are the existing suites too large for the demographic, and if so could you charge similar rents by making three suites into four? What would the cost of making this change be? Does the income that would be gained from the additional suite justify the cost? These are all important questions.

The best kind of suite addition is the one where you can add a suite without disrupting any existing suites – as Robert did in the example above.

Improve Management

One of the best gifts a multi-family investor can ever receive is the gift of a poorly managed property.

Taking over a poorly managed property might seem like a nightmare, but there is a huge opportunity to improve valuation simply by raising rents in undermanaged buildings. Adding value through better management brings an exponential ROI since the changes made by the new landlord *cost nothing*.

The most common change in management standards is to simply raise rents. Lazy landlords often don't keep their rents up to market level, which gives the new landlord an immediate opportunity to raise the value (by raising the rents).

The second most common change is to market the property more aggressively, thereby shortening vacancy times. Anything landlords can do to keep rents at market value and shorten vacancy times will make a huge impact on the valuation.

A third common management improvement professional real estate investors use to raise valuation is through turnover (and renovation) efficiencies. Every time there is a suite turnover there is the opportunity to get the suite re-tenanted immediately. The best property managers aim to have zero days in between one tenant exiting and the next entering. This raises the question as to when you do renovations. Well, the best managers do everything in their power to work around the difficulty of doing renovations as tenants are moving in and out.

If the suite needs to be painted, one strategy is to get the outgoing tenant let your wall repair crew into the suite in advance of the painting day. They fill all the holes and nicks in the wall so that the filler is dry on time for the painting crew, which can come in and paint all the walls in half a day.[5]

Minimizing vacancies is one way operational efficiency improves valuation, but the greatest professionals take this to the furthest degree by developing key performance indicators (KPIs). For example, Boardwalk measures their rental income per suite against the rental market as a whole. They have a range where they want to be in relation to the rental market.

Learn about these metrics, measure them, and use them to improve your performance.

---

5 A tip of the cap: to Quentin D'Souza for explaining tips and efficiencies for moving tenants in and out without vacancies.

In-Suite Renovations

Shabby properties attract lower rents and a lower tenant profile. Thus, simply renovating a unit will allow you to raise the rents. I love the idea of doing Christmas presents, but instead of a fruit basket, give them a RONA catalogue with a message that says, "Here's $200 for your suite. What would you like?" Your tenants get something they appreciate; you get a better relationship with your tenants, targeted renovations done, higher rent, and lower turnover.

Renovations are the key to the most common formula for raising rents. Consistent, ongoing, and targeted renovations should be a part of every multi-family real estate investor's strategy.

Curb Appeal

First impressions are everything in real estate. Whether they know it or not, every prospective tenant is asking themselves whether or not the building looks like the kind of place crack addicts would live or if it looks like the kind of building an upstanding citizen would live?

Put yourself in the renter's shoes. What would you think of your building if you saw it from the street? Be honest. If your impression is negative, then you must improve curb appeal to attract better tenants (and therefore improve rents) by making it feel safe and welcoming.

Curb Appeal

First impressions are everything in real estate. Whether they know it or not, every prospective tenant is asking themselves whether or not the building looks like the kind of place crack addicts would live or if it looks like the kind of building an upstanding citizen would live?

Put yourself in the renter's shoes. What would you think of your building if you saw it from the street? Be honest. If your impression is negative, then you must improve curb appeal to attract better tenants (and therefore improve rents) by making it feel safe and welcoming.

The best thing about improving curb appeal is that it's generally simple and cheap.

It's often a simple matter of painting the sign on the front of the building or replacing the numbers beside the door. The parking lot might need to be cleaned, or graffiti might need to be painted over. You can change the tenant's first impression from 'ghetto' to 'upstanding' with very little effort. The reason these changes so often don't get completed is that they're so small and cheap it doesn't seem like it's worth your (or you property manager's) time – but they are.

> *"The things you touch every day should be nice."*
>
> **Calvin Peters**

Common Areas

As with curb appeal, the common areas of a multi-family building form the first impression. Remember that the first impression is the most important, since it arrives in the prospect's unconscious as a feeling. The first impression is likely pre-cognitive. You may not realize this but more decisions are made on the level of unconscious feeling than on the level of conscious thought.

A newly painted entranceway or well-lit laundry room leaves a great first impression. Again, these repairs are generally quite inexpensive. Replacing hallway carpets is probably the only big common area expense. Steam cleaning the carpets (on the other hand) isn't too costly, but it usually produces the same result.

When you take over a poorly managed building, there will often be low-hanging fruit. The small act of cleaning a property usually makes a big difference in common area impression.

Practicing Alchemy

There is no perfect formula for these changes that will yield an exact dollar figure increase to value, but by putting them together, real estate investors increase the value on their properties.

However, the combined effect of small changes resembles an alchemical reaction. By small adjustments, most buildings can be transformed after taking over from a bad landlord.

Incentives, Additional Fees, and the Effect on Valuation

An investor friend named CJ loves cooking up imaginative ways to increase income across his portfolio. He never ceases to amaze me with his creative ideas for raising income. One of the ways he's creative is with incentives and fees. He places a high value on receiving rent on time, so he utilizes an incentive system with his tenants to ensure rents are on time.

If a tenant pays rent on time they get a $50 discount for the month. Now, calling it a discount is just a positive way to frame what is really a penalty for late payment. CJ prices his rent intentionally high, and it is only by receiving the 'discount' that rent comes back down to market level.

This works for him because many tenants feel they're getting a great deal just for paying rent on time. If by chance the tenant pays late the landlord has a built in fee for late rental payment (the normal rent).

CJ also has several different ways to charge *additional fees*. For example:

1. Premium parking spaces cost more than a normal parking space.
2. He rents additional parking spaces.
3. He charges higher rent to smokers in some buildings.
4. He charges a monthly fee to small pet owners (he even offers a dog walking service that he has hired a local teenager to run for an additional fee).

These are just a sample of what is possible. Creative investors like CJ never tire of finding new ways to profit. Donald Trump made millions off just the billboards and other advertising on his buildings. There's many a landlord who has hosted cell phone towers, vending machines and meeting spaces. The extra cash is great, but the valuation growth that comes along with the higher income is even better.

However, I need to warn you about using additional fee and penalty structures. The problem with additional fees and incentives comes in the bookkeeping and tracking process. If you're not fastidious about keeping records on these things and having them in the lease, then you will run into problems getting the additional income included in your valuation for financing.

Banks and CMHC are risk averse. When they see creative fees they sometimes automatically assume the investor is doing something illegal or earning illegitimate income. All extra income should be in writing and clearly explainable.

Without including the extra income in the valuation, the greater part of value ends up being left on the table. Imagine a 20-suite building where each suite earns $50 above market rent in additional fees. This amounts to $12,000 additional income per year. The value increase from extra fees on such a property would be $200,000 at a 6% cap rate. In other words, the value growth is more valuable than the additional cash.

The valuation growth is only achievable, though, if all additional fees are properly accounted for. Excellent bookkeeping is often the difference between thriving in business or not, so be systematic and thorough when tracking additional fees or penalties. Without being clear on this you won't receive the full benefit of the additional cash.

An additional warning: if additional fees are a big part of your business model you must also be prepared for the risk that (even if you track it perfectly) some banks won't count your additional fees towards a valuation. Some banks just don't play that game.

Therefore, the best strategy for additional fees is to include them *within* the lease. If it's part of the actual rent (and you can show the leases as proof) then it's a heck of a lot harder for a lender to deny you.

Capital Expenses vs. Operational Expenses – The Long Term Picture

New multi-family investors are often unaware that accounting practices are somewhat fluid. I'd like to warn you that I'm not advocating cooking the books, nor am I an accountant. What I'm saying is that accounting practices are often open to interpretation. This gives investors a bit of flexibility as to how they do accounting during different phases of ownership.

Accounting fluidity ultimately comes down to operational expenses vs. capital expenses.

Depending how you manage your accounting, you can affect valuation dramatically. There are two different methods of accounting, and you will need to employ both depending on the phase of ownership you're in.

To explain we need to do a brief explanation of the two types of expense:

1. **Operational Expense:** An operational expense is something necessary for the day-to-day operations of the building. The onsite manager's salary or fixing a drippy tap are examples of operational expenses.

    We need to spend this money just to keep the building operating, yet there is no real long-term benefit – no lasting value – once the expense is paid.

    Operational expenses are part of the regular churn of the property and are deducted from income, which decreases your tax bill.

2. **Capital Expenditure:** A capital expenditure, on the other hand, provides an enduring benefit and is considered the equivalent of adding assets to your holdings. Capital expenditures are depreciated over the life of their value. An example of this would be renovating the bathroom, rather than just fixing the tap.

    When a road construction company purchases a new bulldozer with a value of $300,000 and it's depreciated at 10 per cent yearly. So the bulldozer's value would drop to $270,000 at the end of the first year.

The money spent by the road construction company to purchase the bulldozer will be claimed as a capital expenditure. The company spends cash but adds a real asset.

In real estate capital expenditures are those items that are perceived to have lasting value to the owner.

Using these two types of expense claims we can develop two different accounting strategies to match the phase the investor is currently in.

First, there is *ownership phase accounting*. During this time, multi-family investors seek to minimize their yearly tax bill. In order to minimize taxes we claim every possible expense as operational. If we have a $60,000 bill coming up to replace all of the windows in a bigger building, then we will try to claim every penny possible as operational expense.

In truth, CRA would never let us get away with that. Windows are more of a capital expense. Still, there would be some opportunity to claim at least part of this as an operational expense or at least a strong argument to spread it out over a couple years.

There are more mundane examples. For example, every investor has a yearly plumbing expense. Toilets break, drains get clogged, and there are plenty of other times when the plumbers are called in. This is the nature of the business. The lawn needs to be cut and the snow needs to be removed. These are purely operational expenses.

During the normal ownership period you will seek to make all of your expenditures operational expenses because it reduces your tax bill.

The second phase is more strategic. Let's call this second phase the *sale preparation phase.* Here, you *purposefully spend more on capital expenses* than during the ownership phase. This will result in a higher tax bill but will help raise the value of the property in advance of the sale. You're trading a few thousand in higher taxes for several thousand in future sale value. Remember, $1,000 in net income becomes $16,666 in value at a 6 per cent cap rate.

By claiming higher capital expenditures you show greater NOI on the balance sheet. It's a simple equation: higher NOI = higher valuation. The trick is to prepare for the sale at the right time to strike the right balance between taxes and valuation. The idea is that by spending the extra money at the right time you bring rents up and monthly expenses down, thereby improving the NOI.

In other words, it's not enough to randomly spend more money on capital expenditures. Each expense must increase income or decrease expense. Whereas a new boiler won't help you raise incomes, it might reduce your energy cost for each unit.

Each expense must be analyzed on a case-by-case basis to see if the additional tax expense would be more than made up in higher valuation. If the new boiler lowers energy expense by $50 per month across 20 units it would amount to a yearly NOI improvement of $12,000, which amounts to just under $200,000 of valuation at a 6 per cent cap rate.

Executing this strategy has other benefits, too. Building upgrades help reduce expenses. For example, new windows are more energy efficient, which brings energy bill savings.

Furthermore, *improving the building* will always help achieve a higher price. Even prospective multi-family buyers like shiny and new, since it reduces the risk they'll have a large cash call later.

The normal holding phase strategy is distinctively different than the sale preparation phase strategy. It's sometimes hard for investors to wrap their heads around the notion of *spending more* money on taxes, when they're normally geared toward expense minimization.

Humans are simple creatures. It takes heavy thinking to grasp the longer term and the bigger picture. Simplistic rules of thumb that work on one scale don't always work on a different scale.

Real estate investors succeed because they learn to be frugal, trying not to spend money wherever possible. Paying taxes erodes wealth every single year, so we wisely develop strategies to minimize tax expense.

But humans often apply rules dogmatically without taking into account the bigger picture. We sometimes don't immediately comprehend that paying more taxes might be a good thing. Well, it is a good thing when it comes time to sell so long as the increased valuation more than makes up for the higher tax expense.

At times paying more taxes could mean an exponential increase in valuation for sale time. Would $50,000 of taxes be worth $500,000 more in the sale of a property? This is possible if correctly planned.

> ### Replacing Windows, Spending Money, Raising Value
>
> Recently, we helped a client of mine sell an apartment building in one of Edmonton's working class neighborhoods. Let's take a look at the listing numbers:
>
> $2,250,000 = $115,000/5.111% cap rate
>
> We aimed to be strictly accurate about the NOI numbers and reasonable about the proposed cap rate. The sellers agreed with us and the final sale price was $2.2 million – a mere $50,000 reduction off the sale price.
>
> The sellers were wise, though. They assessed their building prior to sale and did the correct pre-sale prep. In this case, it meant installing $17,000 worth of new windows. This improved their valuation in two ways:
>
> 1. The renovation raised the quality of the building. When negotiating with the buyer they were able to make a strong case that the list price was strong. The buyer knew that the largest expense was already paid for and was therefore happy to pay a higher price.

2. Every penny of the cost of the windows was treated as a capital expense. As a result, the seller's NOI remained strong. If they had chosen to try some of that cost as operational expense, it would have lowered the NOI, thereby lowering the valuation. The big capital expense on windows in the final year of ownership was a strategically smart move even though taxes were a bit higher than normal. The bump in sale price more than made up for the higher tax bill

CHAPTER 7

Value Chain Strategy – Land and Zoning

> *"No matter how good you are, you're going to lose one-third of your games. No matter how bad you are, you're going to win one third of your games. It's the other third that makes the difference."*
>
> Tommy Lasorda

Long Term Strategic Play

Real estate investors love baseball analogies. In real estate, a 'single' is a good deal, a 'homerun' is a great deal, and a 'grand slam' is an otherworldly deal. Like a good baseball team, a good real estate investor wins by hitting several singles rather than swinging for one homerun.

The irony of focusing on singles is that every now and then a homerun or grand slam pitch comes down the plate. One of a pro investor's goals is to be positioned to hit a home run if that happens. Most professional investors have experienced this. A homerun is a (deserving) gift when it does happen. Amateurs search for homeruns and end up striking out more often.

Think of the opposite of a professional baseball player. Imagine a five-year-old kid at his first day of tee-ball. The ball is (literally) teed-up. It's not moving, yet the little guy can't even hit the stationary ball. In his desire to hit the ball far he takes his eye off the target and misses completely.

It's the same with amateur investors. In their lust for a homerun they miss out on great opportunities for a single that would help them win at the real estate game.

The Power of Time

Singles have a compounding effect when lumped together. Each one works in conjunction with the one before it and the sum total is greater than the parts. As with real baseball it's the team with the most runs that wins not the team with the most homeruns.

Time provides the same function in real estate. Singles turn into runs over time because cash flow and valuations grow as markets go up and mortgage payments go down. Results that may seem marginal at first are compounded over time.

Professionals Hit Grand Slams, Too

Turning a single (or even a homerun) into a grand slam requires time plus strategy, which is what an Edmonton investor named Timothy (not his real name) has done. Timothy is a true professional that focuses on solid singles every time he buys a multi-family building. He's been in the business a long time – succeeding with consistent solid efforts.

But Timothy keeps the possibility of a grand slam open every time he purchases property because he *buys strategically and considers the long-term strategic options that* the property might produce.

Timothy has a strong niche. He doesn't buy 'real estate'. He buys a specific type of property in a specific part of town, and he targets a specific demographic of tenants.

Thus, he receives all the benefits discussed in the previous chapter – operations simplification, scales of economy, improved branding and marketing. These are great, but he also keeps open the prospect of a grand slam over the long run. If circumstance plays out well he can cash in on this grand slam later.

Here's what he does: he buys most of his buildings in the same neighborhood and has the chance to do any of the following:

a. Purchase two lots side-by-side.

b. Buy a building beside one of his existing buildings.

c. Add an additional floor to one of his existing buildings.

The result of any of these strategic plays is that Timothy adds a bunch of units to his properties several years after buying when cash flow is more abundant and debt is reduced. This often happens a decade or more after the initial purchase.

It makes sense as development ideology. After all, it's far cheaper to add rental units where existing infrastructure is in place than to start with fresh dirt. Where there are two buildings on side-by-side lots, Timothy sometimes knocks down both buildings and builds a single building with more rental units than the two smaller buildings combined.

Or, he simply adds a floor to an existing building. For example, he recently added a fourth floor to a 15-unit three-story walk-up building in Edmonton. By adding five suites at a value of $120,000 per door Timothy raised the building's value by $600,000. A $1.8 million building became a $2.4 million building. Of course, there were construction costs. He achieved this value lift for a build cost of about $525,000, which he financed with equity built up in the property over the 10 years of ownership.

It's an immediate equity growth of $75,000 without spending a penny of his money. Not bad, but the benefits don't end there as it's also a huge cash-flow boost and future value boost. For every $1000 in rising per suite value, he's now grown his net worth by $20,000 (on that building) rather than $15,000. This is called a grand slam. Strategic investors like Timothy do this. It's how folks build serious wealth.

There are other benefits of this strategy. For starters, doing this helps put more units under the management of a single onsite manager. This is vitally important if you have a great onsite manager. Professional multi-family investors do what they can to leverage the efforts of great onsite managers.

Value Chain Strategy – Land and Zoning

Professionals Don't Risk the Single for the Grand Slam

Here's the thing about professional investors: they don't risk losing the single for the grand slam. If Timothy's 10-year vision to build additional suites is never realized he will still be wildly successful just based on the singles.

He still concentrates his buildings in the same geographic areas for all of the reasons we discuss in this book (marketing, operations, branding, etc.). He still buys buildings side-by-side, knowing that even if he never combines them he'll still make a ton of money and reap a ton of benefits by their proximity.

Timothy also doesn't pass up a building across the street if it fits his other criterion simply because he'll never be able to add suites later. Timothy is a professional, so he sets himself up to win in any case. As a professional, he also remains aware of future possibilities for grand slams.

This is just one component of the land and zoning strategy that professional investors consider during the acquisition phase. It's part of an overall strategy to win during purchase, optimization and disposition.

Land and Zoning Considerations in Acquisition Phase

One of the basic facts about land is that it's fixed in place. You can't move your land somewhere else. Zoning is nearly as fixed, since the forces of bureaucracy are nearly as rigid.

I'm only partially kidding. Changing zoning is a deep and detailed process.

It's detailed and not easy, but changing zoning to develop more units is a task perfectly suited to a creative, professional real estate investor. Doing it early in your real estate investing career is too complex for most, but every investor should at least keep an eye on the future potential of their assets through the lens of zoning.

Investors have two land and zoning based considerations in the acquisition phase:

1. Mitigating risk posed by the land or the zoning of a target property.

2. Thinking strategy about future land and zoning rewards. Purchase a property that works as-is what, but being able to change (for example) the zoning from RA7 to RA9 leads to the possibility of that incredible future payday. It's the kind of money that could change a family's intergenerational trajectory. Zoning can do that.

Using Land and Zoning to Niche-Up

Can the land a building sits on (or zoning opportunities it contains) help deepen your presence in a niche? To answer this question we need to consider the various ways business is improve by niche focus. Let's take a look at some of the ways land and zoning can be considered in the niche-building exercise:

1. **Branding:** Having a brand means first knowing what causes pain for a prospect.

Value Chain Strategy – Land and Zoning

In real estate, this means that whenever there is a group of people with a specific problem, there is opportunity to profit by providing housing that suits the needs of the group of people with the problem.

The City of St. Albert is fostering a niche for developers in Edmonton that has applied deep brand thinking by focusing developments around the northwest corner of St. Albert – a bedroom community of Edmonton. They have built a brand that includes the idea of a 'clean air' housing development, as there is no cleaner air anywhere in Edmonton than in the northwest corner of St. Albert.

This position solves a problem in the buyer's mind and is unforgettable.

It's the kind of thing buyers get attached to. They want to be associated with clean air and others that value clean air. Sure, it's a small part of a larger campaign, but for families with respiratory problems it'll take the competition out of the picture.

Land and zoning won't play a huge role in every niche, but this is a perfect example of selecting a niche based on the land.

An example more appropriate to multi-family investors is to own a brand as the rental community of choice around the new arena development in Edmonton or as a premium brand catering to downtown office workers.

2. **Marketing** – The brand supports marketing efforts. You might even say there is no effective marketing without a brand. Marketing without brand is spasmodic, painful, and never-ending.

   The development company with the 'clean air' brand knows exactly what to say over and over again in its marketing efforts.

   Downtown apartment buildings can do marketing based on the location of land as well. High-rise apartment towers can market as the uptown, hip, and urban option. This is made possible by the zoning of the building. The three-story walk-up will always have a hard time marketing itself as upscale, but it can appeal to a less-flashy community-based set of people that like walkability and ambiance.

   Zoning matters. It's key to find opportunities to capitalize on zoning.

3. **Specialization and Opportunity:** The 'brownfield' development craze has been underway in cities like Montreal for several years now, and just recently it has hit the city of Edmonton. 'Brownfields' are a relic of our industrial past when warehouses and factories sat beside our commercial centers.

   Turning these 'brownfields' into residential housing has been a boon for many creative real estate investors. They have taken a specific type of land with a specific type of zoning and developed a specialization out of it.

Value Chain Strategy –Land and Zoning

The typical pattern (of developing specialization) is to spruce up existing buildings while holding for development to sweep through the neighbourhood – at this point the grand slam moment comes where the property's zoning can be converted to a much higher and better use (for example, building a high rise where a warehouse once was).

A Zoning Quagmire

Zoning is both a huge opportunity and a massive risk. By changing the zoning of a parcel of land, the value is raised significantly. However, some zonings scenarios make a property almost un-saleable. This is the risky side of zoning.

Recently, I listed a commercial property with CB2 zoning. This is about the best zoning possible, as the owner can operate (or lease to) any kind of commercial business on the site. A week after listing it I noticed the property next door – which was almost exactly the same – was also listed.

I was shocked and a little upset to see that it was listed for about half the price of my listing. I thought I'd either gotten my value analysis horribly wrong or that the other building realtor was incompetent. I thought there was no way my listing would sell until the other one sold first and that our prospects for a good sale price were gone – until I checked the zoning of the other building. This property was zoned 'urban services', as it was an old Canada Post location.

> Essentially, with its existing zoning the building could only be used by government offices. The government had already abandoned the site and had no intention of coming back, which left the owner in a precarious position.
>
> The zoning of the property ended up being an obstacle to selling the building. Whoever takes a chance on buying it will have to deal with the work of changing zoning. If they're able to solve the problem they will then get a huge boost in value. At that point, the building may become a homerun.
>
> Wherever there is risk, there is also opportunity. Zoning provides a chance to move up the value-chain exponentially as long as it doesn't sink you in the meantime.

CHAPTER 8

The Value Chain Strategy – Operations

> *"Efficiency is doing things right; effectiveness is doing the right things."*
>
> Peter Drucker

Where You Set Yourself Apart

Amateur investors often love the romantic view of real estate, of the independent man or woman wheeling, dealing, and doing cool stuff with all their newfound free time. When they think of real estate their minds settles on acquisitions and lifestyle.

I'm not suggesting acquisition isn't important – obviously it is. I'm suggesting that acquisition alone is not enough. The (perhaps) more important component to real estate success – to building a legacy – is operations.

When people see a painting by Henri Matisse, they see pure genius at work. Few people stop to consider the boring, repetitive hours Matisse had to spend mastering his brush stroke, developing a deft touch with his fingers, studying the shapes of things, and even time spent staring at things. People see the end result, or perhaps they see the romantic side of Matisse's life – days and years spent lingering in the countryside of France. They don't see the drool inducing boredom of repeating the same movements millions of times.

Of course, it wasn't boring to Matisse.

He got the result because he was willing to lean into the boredom. Real estate investors need to develop the same ability. You don't get to experience the fun of the lifestyle or the excitement of acquisitions unless you master the boredom of operations.

The amateur answer is, "I'll outsource management." This is a good strategy, but outsourcing does not relieve the investor from responsibility. There will always be a measure of tedium in some tasks. The investor still has to figure it out. Avoiding or ignoring the problem doesn't make it go away.

As Seth Godin says:

> *"We know what you want to accomplish. We know how you'd like everything to turn out.*
>
> *The real question is, "what are you willing to push through the dip for?" What are you willing to stand up for, bleed for, commit to and generally be unreasonable about?*
>
> *Because that's what's going to actually get done."*

The Value Chain Strategy – Operations

Amateur investors rarely foresee the operational grind of owning several multi-family real estate properties.

When an investor does operations well you almost never hear much about it. Yet, poor operations are behind most spectacular multi-family investing failures. Building a ship and sailing it across the ocean are different.

Operations are the unspectacular, every day execution component of real estate investing. If there is one real estate truth not spoken often enough it's that operational excellence wins the real estate journey. An oft-spoke truism of real estate is that you make the money when you buy the property.

This is true, but poor management can easily lose the same money.

Lots of people ask me about various asset classes and REIN had a chart that said the average appreciation between the usual single family/condo classes was 8 to 10 per cent. Not bad, right? Great management can help a property do much better than average.

There is a very real element of forced appreciation from excellent operations.

Investors must delegate as much as possible. Neglect and delegation are not the same. Every strategic decision in real estate investing is the owner's decision. There is no way around this fact, yet the myth of 'passive income' continues.

Owners have the hardest job of all – thinking and executing.

Amateur investors assume the hard part (operations) is the easy part, and the easy part (acquisition) is the hard part, so they have backwards priorities.

> ## The 5-Point Delegation Plan
>
> 1. **Determine what is to be delegated**
> 2. **Identify the right person**
> 3. **Assign the task**
> 4. **Monitor progress**
> 5. **Evaluate performance**
>
> By going through this exact process several times, your operations will improve incrementally over time. Just as with hitting real estate singles, there is a compounding effect of delegation successes. Failing to use this process will cause continued poor delegation results.[6]
>
> ---
>
> 6 http://realbusiness.co.uk/article/26516-5-tips-that-will-teach-you-how-to-delegate-effectively

The Value Chain Strategy – Operations

Operational Effectiveness – The Boardwalk Example

Boardwalk is an institutional investor focused on the Alberta market that demonstrates boring but effective operations. I actually regard this company as a pioneer of effective operations.

Not having access to the strategic conversations in the boardroom I can only speculate based on what I see externally. Based on appearances it seems as though Boardwalk purposely gets in front of demographic trends. Once their properties are in the path of the trend, they then tailor their system to corner this market.

Boardwalk established itself at a time (in the early 90s) when Edmonton's three largest post-secondary institutions were undergoing big growth phases (they still are).

Operationally, they did something that was revolutionary at the time. Knowing that their target demographic (students) were early online adopters they invested big in their website. It was the operational implementation of a strategic-seeming (I can only speculate) thought-process.

This might seem mundane, but keep in mind that the Internet landscape was a lot different back then.

At the time, students were the most Internet savvy consumers around. Even if you didn't have an Internet connection and computer at home, every student had access to a computer and the Internet through their school.

I'll never forget Boardwalk's website from that time because it was much better than the others. The biggest innovation was an interactive map on the website that showed where the available units for rent were located. It also included photos and descriptions of units for rent.

We have become so accustomed to the Internet conveniences that we've forgotten how revolutionary interactive maps were. Boardwalk had an interactive map on its website four years before Google Maps was launched. This technology must have been expensive for Boardwalk, but it was so much better than the competition that it created an operational advantage for the company. They still reap the benefits of that advantage.

Credit goes to Boardwalk's executive team for green-lighting what must have been an expensive and perhaps difficult to understand project (especially for gray-haired boardroom sitters).

We'll probably never know if it was a strategic plan or a fortunate accident, but let's step back and take a wider view at exactly what Boardwalk did:

1. **Get in Front of a Demographic Trend:** The school (student and staff) populations were growing rapidly when Boardwalk started accumulating assets around all of the major post-secondary institutions. They were developing and improving their niche. *This is vital for serving long-term operational needs.*

2. **They Tailored Their Operations to Suit Their Demographic** – One of the most important reasons for having detailed niche is that operations can be streamlined.

With Boardwalk's niche focus they were able to tailor their efforts to their target renter – the online student demographic.

The website must have paid for itself several times over by creating a smooth path to bring renters in the door. Imagine how many phone calls were avoided once the website was operational.

Having Data-Driven Operations Systems

The Boardwalk example is instructive in showing the link between niche and how operations can be streamlined, but let's face it: Boardwalk is a large entity. Can smaller investors achieve similar results in a niche?

Results will vary, but there is a lesson to be learned from the bigger guys that smaller multi-family investors can apply. Successful institutional scale investors are *data-driven*. Now, you might be thinking that being data-driven is a luxury only available to the biggest of players, but this couldn't be further from the truth.

Sure, billion-dollar public companies analyze data in a way smaller firms can't replicate. They apply lease-rate-optimization software and complex property management tracking systems. Big firms have the luxury of being able to employ economists and statisticians. With these differences, it's not wise to try replicating the big guys' mass data-driven approach, but smaller investors can approximate it and use the same principles. Every investor must pay attention to data.

The big, institutional-level players have the distinct advantage of being able to collect data on a much larger scale. Their sample sizes have *statistical relevance,* which means they have a large enough data set to ensure their sample is meaningful. Smaller players don't have this advantage, which means we, a) must be selective about the kind of data we collect, and b) rely on broad data carried out by larger entities. This still doesn't replace data from our exact units, but it can be a great approximation.

Smaller players can't collect larger sample sizes, so we need to collect more specific data and look for overwhelming feedback on a specific issue.

Out-of-town investors are often forced into such data collection. Not having the advantage of being on the ground, they often develop a more systematic approach to operations, and I find they often use data to drive policy, even on small scales.

Darlene is an investor I know from Ontario that invests in Edmonton. One of Darlene's properties is a package of 15 carriage-style homes in the Castledowns area of Edmonton.

When one property came up for rent, Darlene was met with an uncomfortable statistical fact: she received zero applications from 10 showings.

This stood out because she knew the market wasn't weak and her carriage-home complex usually receives at least two applications from every five showings. She didn't need a larger sample size to figure out that something was wrong.

Yet, she was far away in Ontario and couldn't figure it out. Her property management was competent, but competency is often a low bar in residential property management. Yes, she could switch property managers, but it wasn't an option until at least after the property was rented, and there was no guarantee that future property management would be any better, so she started thinking about how she could solve the problem. It involved collecting a bit of data.

Darlene's solution was simple, elegant, and useful for smaller investors. She decided to burrow her way into the minds of the decision makers.

She devised a simple index card style feedback form to collect targeted data about the property, and her data collection system was born. On the card were two simple questions:

1. Would you live here?
2. If not, why?

She instructed her property manager that the cards were to be put in a box on the way out the door. This way prospects would remain anonymous.

Most people hate conflict so they rarely give negative feedback unless they know it will be anonymous. People tell their friends bad things about an apartment or restaurant, but they rarely tell the people who could actually do something about it. The only way to elicit negative feedback is to make it easy and anonymous.

The property manager then continued showing the property. Again, they showed it to 10 prospects in a couple of days, and again none of the prospects applied to live in the carriage home, but this time the property manager captured six feedback forms. He sent an email with the responses to Darlene.

Four out of the six feedback forms mentioned that the price seemed high for the quality of the property. Darlene knew this wasn't the case because she was renting other similar properties for similar price. The feedback forced her to think harder. She surmised three things from this feedback:

1. **The Property Needed Some Sprucing Up.** When renting a higher end rental product, the prospects need to feel like they're getting something nicer than the typical rental.

   Darlene looked for more detailed feedback from her property manager and found that this particular suite was the only one of her 15 that had outdated paint colors and older style trim. She wasn't previously aware of this. The property manager could have told her but wasn't thinking like a tenant. Now that she knew, she could take the appropriate action.

2. **The Prospects Needed to be Educated.** The carriage home complex had several advantages that many of the tenants weren't aware of. Snow removal on the sidewalks, for example, was included in the price of rent. There were a few other high-end features that the tenants weren't being made aware of.

The Value Chain Strategy – Operations

Darlene found out that there was an internal changeover in her property management company, and although she'd provided feature sheets for tenant turnovers they weren't being used in this case.

She re-instituted the use of feature sheets immediately to ensure prospects would be properly educated to the advantages of the property.

3. **The Advertising Needed to Be More Focused.** The property management company was using a shotgun approach to advertising. Instead of targeting the correct tenant type they were advertising randomly. As a result, they ended up with the wrong kind of prospects.

The advertising was playing to someone looking for a great deal. When their expectations for the property didn't match what they thought was a deal they simply walked.

With this knowledge, Darlene did some more research into the perfect tenant type. Darlene learned by researching her current tenants that just under 50 per cent were military.

She knew that military members prize convenience and like to be located near their base.

Darlene asked her property management if the military base was being targeted in advertising and found it wasn't, so she made sure her listing appeared in the next edition of the on-base paper.

Based on her data and analysis, Darlene was able to make immediate changes with immediate results. Until then she received zero applications from 12 showings. After making the changes she received six applications from 14 showings.

What a difference a little data makes.

The data is important, but Darlene's analysis was as important (or more) to this success story. Smaller investors can't collect data like the big guys, but they can collect super-focused data and use it to draw excellent conclusions.

The secret to doing this well is to know your client well. Imagine a small neighborhood grocery store that specializes in artisanal meats and cheeses versus a big grocery store chain. The artisanal market has many disadvantages, but they have the opportunity to develop a close relationship with clients.

The artisanal market owner/operator can stock meats and cheeses their clients love, and they can delight their clients with new and interesting products. They can learn about wine in order to discuss and recommend wines to accompany the meats and cheeses they purchase. They can even open a wine shop next to the artisanal market to serve the peripheral wine needs of the client. Attempting to compete with the big supermarket chain down the road would be self-destructive for the artisanal shop owner.

A smaller business can develop a specialized niche based on superior knowledge of a smaller group of people. Boardwalk is a big company, and can use big data for a bigger niche. Smaller investors need to use more contextualized data to target a more specific niche.

Darlene was brilliant to target military renters. A carriage home appeals to a different market than a typical apartment building, and as the owner of such a complex she had to target her efforts more.

Using data with strong analysis can be a powerful tool to move up the value chain.

Amateur Operations Don't Scale

Real estate investors commonly face the problem of scalability. Growing multi-family investors have to think about scale at some point. Having a niche makes this easier.

Scaling operations is especially important as a portfolio grows. Every real estate investor wants to scale up holdings. However, few understand the need to scale operations alongside holdings. Having enough capacity is vital. Failed operations systems have sunk more real estate investors than any other problem (with the exception of over-leveraging). Failing to scale is actually another kind of over-leveraging. It's the equivalent of trying to overleverage a weak system.

An amateur Edmonton investor (who shall remain nameless) epitomizes this problem. He is the wheeler-dealer type, which is a vital skill for acquisitions. He can talk with the best of them and he closes plenty of business. I give him full credit for his strengths.

However, he suffers from the hubris that many wheeler-dealers do. He assumes that sales skills translate to operational skill, and he approaches operations in the same way he approaches making deals, looking for cheap deals with every operational situation that arises, as though it will never happen again.

With operations the best solution isn't always a one of a kind deal. The best solution often requires a systematic fix. When a problem comes up for this investor he runs to the property to solve it. This isn't scalable behavior, but it works perfectly well when you own your first few properties. However, this investor has now moved into multi-family (and he owns several buildings).

I saw a great example of this unscalable operations system as I was driving by one of his properties recently. In the front of the building there was an overgrown spruce tree. It's wise to prune or remove overgrown trees as they can be blown over in big windstorms, causing damage to siding, roofs and balconies and increasing landscaping costs (and injury or death in a worst case scenario).

This investor was having the tree removed – a wise idea. However, the execution was so bad that it created a potentially huge liability.

There are several excellent tree-removal services in Edmonton. These experts not only know how to bring down a large tree without causing any damage, they also have the proper equipment to clean up the mess left behind by the tree. Most importantly, they are insured and bonded, so on the off chance that a falling tree causes damage to property or worse (injury or death) then the owner of the property won't be held liable.

One is not afforded the same level of protection when hiring (for example) a neighborhood teenager. But, this is exactly what the investor in question did. The sad reality is that if the teenager was to fall and die, then all of this investor's success could be wiped out in a single court case.

He would rightfully be found liable for causing the death of a teenager. In such an event, all his properties would be lost, his assets taken away, and his joint venture partners' assets along with them. I don't know about you, but this isn't the kind of joint venture partner I'm looking to invest my money with.

Those things all suck, but the loss of money and assets would be nothing compared to the knowledge that your irresponsibility had killed a teenager. It's simply not worth it to operate this way. If you have any hope of growing beyond the most limited scope you have to think scalability. Small time thinking doesn't suffice as you grow.

This is only an extreme example, of course. Irresponsibility is only one kind of unscalable operational behavior. It's more common for a real estate investor's unscalable operation system to expose them to the dangers of compounding small problems. Let's take a look at how this most often happens:

1. **Lack of niche:** Plenty of investors think their niche is 'Edmonton' or 'apartment buildings'. If only one thing sticks with you from this book I hope it's that your niche needs to be more specific than this. Small scale thinking causes investors to buy randomly, thinking they can run their operation like they always have, but failing to focus on a niche makes operations difficult.

2. **Scrambled Renovations Plan:** Investors can get away with unplanned renovations when running a small operation, but this behavior is unscalable on even a minimally larger scale.

   Use the same paint every time. Buy in bulk. Know which renovations you're going to do before a property ever comes vacant. Book your tradespeople well in advance. Have backups. These are just a few tenets of renovations scalability.

3. **Weak Accounting Practices:** Unfortunately, you sometimes don't know how bad your accounting practices are until long after you should have been improving them.

   There isn't a constant feedback system for this. We only become aware of our bad accounting when it comes time to organize for tax season or when paying a tax bill. You think five single family houses are hard to account for?

   Imagine five multi-family buildings. Start scaling your accounting system now and don't ever stop.

The Value Chain Strategy – Operations

Scalability is about planning and preparing for the worst. If there's one thing you can be certain of it's that markets will shift. We can't rely on an ongoing economic boom to solve real estate problems.

When this happens, investors never seem to understand how bad their systems are until the recession hits, and by then it's too late. Scale up your operations, scale often and scale well. Be ready for the bad times (or be swallowed by the economy).

CHAPTER 9

Value Chain Strategy – Physical Building

"Quit yanking my chain!"

Chris Davies

Move Up The Chain

I love studying the moves of successful investors – both individuals and big companies. One of the companies I keep an eye on is Mainstreet Equities (mentioned earlier). Mainstreet does a lot right.

They execute well every single time they put a new property in their portfolio. Without exception or failure, Mainstreet adds value through a systematic set of renovations. The system is a thing of boring beauty. In fact, they're so predictable I can close my eyes and picture it now.

A Mainstreet building has stucco siding with vertical brick columns about 10 feet apart; they cover the stucco between the brick with light grey or beige vinyl siding. The balconies have aluminum railing with glass panels between the railings.

Inside, they always replace the cabinets in the kitchen, install a new countertop, add new light fixtures, and replace light switches and plug-ins. They replace the small finger-flick switches with the thick, new looking rocker light switches.

The bedrooms of a renovated Mainstreet building are never carpeted, and the bathroom always has new hardware, generic grey tile on the floor and surround, and a new vanity. You can even spot their employees on a site tour, almost always in pairs, black zip-up jacket with a logo and a clipboard.

This is a partial list. Mainstreet is typically more thorough then what I've just mentioned. It's the same, every single time.

And it works. Mainstreet has figured out just the alchemical formula to create gold, with the minimum amount of input possible.

It's widely known that renovating a rental property (of any sort) adds value to the property and is a major factor to increasing the rental income, rental demand and value. In addition, having a spiffy property reduces the market's resistance to renting.

It's widely known, yet even the most successful and experienced investors can't explain precisely the formula for adding value and raising rents through renovations. Sadly, there is no handbook that exists anywhere I'm aware

Value Chain Strategy – Physical Building

of that explains exact correlations between a renovations completed and rental increase achieved. Wouldn't it be great if there were? Picture it:

Replace Kitchen Cabinets = + $18.75 monthly rental increase

Replace Bathroom Vanity = + $11.15 monthly rental increase

There is no exact formula, but there are general principles, the first and most important of which is this: *only visible renovations help raise rent.* Try advertising to your targeted tenants about how awesome a new boiler is and you will soon learn that only visible renovations matter.

There are a couple of exceptions to the rule of visible renovations: *if the renovation allows tenants to save money in some other area, then a non-visible renovation may help earn higher rent.* For example, if you can advertise a lower guaranteed power bill, then you may increase rents accordingly.

Another exception is renovations that play on a tenant's emotions. Visible renovations do this all the time, but it's rare that non-visible renovations do this. The emotional reaction is the right brain reaction. Emotional buy-in is different from logical (left brain) justification. One example is to sell the emotion of green energy and justify with cost, "You mean I can afford the green one?" This strategy targets their emotion and buttresses their initial emotional buy-in with justification.

Conscientious tenants will pay a premium for the benefit of feeling good about their green credentials. A solar panel installation on the roof of a property is an example of such a renovation that might allow you to charge higher rent for a non-visible renovation.

It may be non-visible, but an even better strategy would be to find a way to make it visible when marketing. This isn't something you see every day, but you could try something like putting a green power generation display at the entrance of a building or provide an app that shows the power generated by solar.

Any initiative like that plays on the tenant's emotions has a chance to help you raise rents through renovations. The more standard examples, such as the ones we mentioned at the beginning of this chapter, act on the emotion of pride. Nobody wants to live in a run-down dump. There are only so many times you can paint over the same cupboards.

Climbing the value-chain depends on a consistent renovations system. It further depends on whether or not the investor can systemize.

Have you ever started a small renovation project and immediately noticed that much of the time was spent just driving back and forth from the nearest big box renovation store? This is what happens when renovating without a system.

Having a working system means having materials purchased in advance. There will be no need to run back and forth to the store.

Take that systemization one step further. Mainstreet and other major players (through their system and planning) actually bypass local suppliers and go directly to materials manufacturer, which saves them a ton of money.

Value Chain Strategy – Physical Building

Rather than bulk buying from the local big box store, they go directly to the manufacturers in China for the most commonly used items. What do you think is cheaper: buying trim, hardwood flooring and appliances, or getting a container load of these shipped directly to you from the manufacturer?

I know what you're thinking: "Chris, how am I going to put in an order with a manufacturer? I'm not a big enough player to do that." I'm not suggesting you do, though even firms like Rona and Home Depot will cut deals if you're buying in enough bulk. Copying an institutional investor won't work for smaller players. I'm simply suggesting systemization of the process. Imagine calling your contractor and saying, 'just do *an x*', and they know exactly what to do, which colours, fixtures, appliances and flooring. The time and cost saved on coordination adds up quickly.

You may not be able to order from China, but you can use systematic thinking. For example, when repeat buying the same products you can develop relationships with suppliers to lower cost and streamline operations. Suppliers make deals with repeat customers, but this only becomes a possible after developing the system.

On the other hand, maybe you can order direct from China. Alibaba's 2014 IPO may be a sign of new, simpler opportunities for landlords and managers to acquire goods from China.

To capitalize on a system the investor needs to know her exact trim product, her exact paint colour, and all her product specs. Smaller investors can and must systemize in this way to capitalize on their physical building strategy.

But, deals on materials are just one example of opportunities that arise from the thorough systemization of the physical building strategy. Operations opportunities arise also. Take paint for example. By always using the same colour of paint, you can remove the need for any painter to do two coats of paint. Over the years, this will save you thousands on labour and material. Actually, it takes far less than years. You will save thousands with this one change within the first couple of paint jobs.

Systemization in the physical building strategy bleeds into operations. When a tenant calls with a trim problem, you don't need to send your handyman on a wild goose chase to find the proper trim to use. Instead, you simply send him to a storage unit or warehouse where your trim is stored. No shopping. No matching.

Systemization is most important, but we should also mention renovating to the right level. For example, Mainstreet renovates thoroughly but not high-end. They provide tenants with a 'new feeling'. For their target niche a new feeling is more important than high-end. New trumps expensive furnishings across most tenant types. The obvious exception is in luxury rental properties.

Structural Building

A new boiler, roofing, or foundation has never earned a real estate investor another dollar in rent (with a few exceptions), although spending on these capital expenses at the right time (in advance of a sale) can help increase the valuation (as discussed previously).

Value Chain Strategy – Physical Building

Getting stuck with a big-ticket item can be one of the biggest problems you'll encounter as a real estate investor, but the good news is that you can avoid such issues with a little bit of planning. Unforeseeable expensive problems are few and far between, and there is usually advance warning of such problems.

When it comes to big-ticket items, an investor's job is to not get caught with his pants down. This is mostly solved with proper due diligence during the acquisition phase, but it's also a job of planning because even if you don't get stuck with a big-ticket repair at purchase time, you will still likely have to deal with one of these at some point during the building optimization phase.

No investor can expect to completely avoid big-ticket items. In fact, you will likely develop a keen eye for big-ticket items because you'll begin to see them as opportunities. Where other investors run, you will go in with your eyes wide open and see the opportunity in solving a major problem.

Having cash on hand to pay for a big-ticket item is the best thing, but if you don't have the cash, then the next best thing is to finance a big-ticket item at a future date. This just means planning a refinance to coincide with a major building system replacement.

The rule of big-ticket items is simple: don't let them sink you. They should not since they should be easy enough to spot in advance and have sufficient reserves in place. Rooting out such problems is a rudimentary component of multi-family building investing.

Apartment Buildings That Outperform

Being sunk by a big-ticket item is a risk, but the bigger risk (and more common problem) by far is the opposite: amateurs often walk away from excellent opportunities out of fear of the big renovation. A roof is a big deal, and yes, it costs a lot of dough, but this is not a good reason to run away from a deal. It's as dumb as trying to value a building based on someone's list/asking price. Pros accept the problem, see the solution, negotiate the right price, and plan to make the repair when the time is right.

New investors experience much fear when buying, so it's natural that many new investors would run from major system upgrades. What's far more shocking is when long-time building owners still react fearfully of a big-ticket expense. This happens more often than you might think.

It's not uncommon for an owner to *sell a property* simply because they are being faced with a major expense (or three). I can't think of any better proof than that simply purchasing and owning an apartment building doesn't make one a pro-level investor.

Owners that feel they have to sell because of a large renovation have either failed to plan for the expense, been surprised by it, or couldn't handle the task of managing a renovation.

Only an unprepared owner (if they've owned the building for a while) would fail to have a substantial reserve fund – at least enough to cover the big-ticket expense. At the very least, the building should have enough equity in it to be refinanced and use the equity to pay for the renovation. If the building lacks both it's being mismanaged.

Creating Optionality With a Super Power

This phenomenon of amateurism is so rampant that investors have learned to capitalize on it.

There is a company in Edmonton that specializes in re-roofing commercial buildings, especially multi-family buildings. The owner (I'll call him Steve) of this company has built up a nice portfolio of multi-family properties, partially relying on the opportunistic acquisition strategy of buying buildings from owners that can't execute a re-roofing.

His system is simple. When his company is called to give a quote for a new roof on an apartment building, he simply gauges the seller's level of sophistication, frustration level, and ability to pay for a new roof.

Since Steve knows the severity of the problem, he is able to assess how much it would cost him to replace the roof (at cost). He writes up the quote (fairly, so he doesn't lose the work) and waits to hear what the owner is thinking. If the owner wants to hire Steve's company he takes the job.

However, if the owner baulks or appears to be searching for a better deal, then Steve keeps digging, looking for a potential motivation for the owner to sell. If he can find a strong enough motivation then he will write an offer. Steve has purchased buildings for $20,000 off the per-door price of the building in this way.

Sure, he buys other buildings more 'normally' but he recognizes when this strategy works and uses the right tools for it.

This opportunistic buying may seem like a departure from the niche focus we've been discussing, but there is much advantage to keeping oneself open to options and looking for deals. Buying at 25 per cent off is a strategy unto itself, even if the investor finds him or herself spread out geographically and out of niche (within reason). These properties can be sold at a later date and repositioned around a geographic center when the time is right, though a sudden market drop can limit one's options. Profits from an opportunistic buy (and eventual sell) can be rolled into later real estate purchases. It's like the McDonald's example. McDonald's is really a real estate company that sells burgers opportunistically. They churn burger profits into more top-notch real estate and keep growing value.

Think of Monopoly. In the early stages of the game you buy everything. As time goes on you drill down in your niche, as the game winds down, you trade four houses for a hotel (niching further).

When Steve (the opportunistic roofing guy) buys a seemingly random deal it's like the four houses in Monopoly. He can trade them for his version of a hotel when the time is right. He will sell them and 'niche up' when the time is right.

Value Chain Strategy – Physical Building

The other advantage of buying this way is the direct access to motivated and unsophisticated sellers. How would you like the opportunity to be the only buyer offering on a simple value-add deal? This is a dream come true for most pro real estate investors. Steve's system of opportunistic acquisitions is a great tool to supplement his overall strategy, and he serves as a good example for the rest of us.

In this book, we've been discussing strategy a lot. Strategy is important, but there is the opposite risk of over-strategizing and never acting. The best investors have a strategy but aren't afraid to move fast and break things – provided that in the breaking of things they don't break themselves.

Steve has the wherewithal to put the new roof on the property at a fraction of the cost that most can. He's given himself optionality due to a special ability. How can you give yourself optionality? Remember that special abilities can be special relationships. The best investors always seek out ways to tilt the playing field in their favour.

Not everyone will be able to come in and scoop up deals the same way Steve does, but there is much to be learned from his approach. Look for your own investing super power and you may be surprised what you discover.

Apartment Buildings That Outperform

The way you handle the physical building is a huge component of strategic and systematic optimization. As a stand-alone factor, the physical building (and associated improvements) provides the biggest opportunity to add value, raise rents, streamline tenant turnover, improve property desirability, and systematize until your building runs like a top. In simpler words, it's the biggest opportunity to move up the value-chain.

CHAPTER 10
The Solidifying Strategy

"There's no profit or loss until you sell. Until that point it's all academic."

Chris Davies

Disposition

When does one sell to dispose of a property, and when is a sale just a chess move in a larger repositioning strategy? Real estate investors who care about legacy often never really get out of real estate.

Why should they?

The hardest work is done on the front end. Once you have a well-oiled system for operations in place real estate is almost self-operating. I'm not suggesting taking one's eye off the ball. I'm just saying that a working system carries itself forward seamlessly. This is even truer when the investor is no longer making acquisitions and as debt goes ever downward over the long haul.

Once the system is in place, each optimized building is like a gift that keeps on giving. So, holding longer is generally better, but there are occasions when pro investors sell an asset and use the money for something entirely outside of real estate.

However, it's often more strategic to use the disposition as a perfect opportunity to move up the value chain, which is why many real estate investors never truly exit, choosing instead to reposition with each sale. Money makes money by its velocity, and once a building has been fully optimized the investors can gain velocity by either a) selling the building and freeing up more human capital, time and money to buy something better, or b) refinancing the building which is a core asset at the right moment.

You may have heard this strategy phrased like this before: "when the market is hot, it's time to sell your dogs." This is true in a simple sense, but there is a much larger strategic aim at play when carrying out this principle.

Pros are supposed to buy strategically for their niche, aren't they? Why do they have dogs?

The best investors start with a niche and then – using the entrepreneurial process of trial-and-error – they make adjustments mid-stream. Professional investors find they like a certain sub-niche better than another, so they 'niche up' on the fly. A dog is often just a property that doesn't fit one's niche.

The Solidifying Strategy

Moving Up the Value Chain

I've used the phrase value chain throughout this book. Optimizing is the process of moving up the value chain, and every value-creation investor – to be successful – must optimize and move up the value chain.

An investor named Dave first introduced the concept of moving up the value chain to me. In reality, he just gave me a fluent way to think and talk about the process of adding value over the lifetime of building ownership. Great investors do it, but I'd never thought of it as a chain, which has an end. I like this visualization because when the end of the chain is reached the investor must make a decision about what to do with the property.

Dave told me he has a clear value chain in place from the day he purchases a property. His job is to maximize the value of a property with his very clear, step-by-step system for operations and physical building optimization.

Once that system has been executed, the building's value production velocity slows down. Everything is working well at that point, which means the value has been raised about as much as it can be (excepting market appreciation).

At this point Dave asks himself a serious question: "Do I use this optimized asset to increase velocity by repositioning or refinancing? Or should I just sit and let the time and the market do their thing."

We will call this decision and how an investor executes it the *solidifying strategy*. The point is to be strategic about moving assets around and/or not moving them around. If the goal is a stronger and stronger portfolio over time, then deeper niche penetration is the goal. To achieve this, investors must continue to be strategic during this phase.

So what does it look like to be, 'optimized to the top of the value chain'?

Once the building's expenses are as low as is possible at the moment and the incomes as high as possible, the physical building is in top shape, and the building's value raised as much as possible (via all the strategies), then the top of the value chain has been reached.

Being at the top of the value chain provides the best opportunity to use the building as a chess piece in a larger reposition. An investor might have learned via real time feedback that he or she doesn't actually like owning a specific asset since it's not part of his or her larger strategy.

Not loving the asset is even more reason to put all resources available into a full speed climbing of the value chain, since knowing it's not the right asset means you will be selling to reposition. For it to be an effective chess piece in a repositioning move, the asset has to be optimized to the very top of the value-chain.

Selling can help reposition, but it's not necessary to sell every time. If the building is in your niche then by all means it's a great idea to keep it. Long-term appreciation is still the special sauce that makes real estate great. The goal of holding for appreciation is only secondary to the goal of hanging in there for legacy. Remember that legacy requires a portfolio built to stand the test of time.

The Solidifying Strategy

Dave keeps plenty of great buildings once they are at the top of the value chain. Where he differs from a lot of amateurs is in holding dogmatically. Selling is okay – it's not an admission of failure.

If you buy a building in-niche then you will be perfectly positioned to increase the velocity of money at the top of the value chain with a refinance rather than a sale. The refinance is a slight reposition, not as extreme as selling to buy more in-niche.

Knowing the optimization phase will raise value and income, plenty of pro investors don't take out long-term cheap money right away. Why get a long-term mortgage on a much lower value?

Better off to consider that the optimization phase will take a year or two and plan for the term of short-term money to expire just as the optimization phase ends.

On one level we're just playing with semantics here. I've been saying the refinance is part of the solidifying strategy (which may be a reposition, refinance, or hold as is), but in cases of refinancing, one might consider it the final step of optimization.

But I like considering the refinance to be part of the solidifying strategy because it builds the idea that the refinancing decision will be made after deciding if the building is firmly in-niche or not.

Either way you slice it, a refinance can be part of a significant move up the value chain, and it has the benefit of avoiding the cost of selling, which can be significant. Rather than using the sale of a building to increase the velocity of money, a refinance achieves the same goal while keeping the asset in the long-term wealth-creation zone, which should be a goal for investors. Selling can lock in profit for an investor, and that's important, but the long-term (where appreciation and mortgage pay down happen) are the real bread and butter of residential real estate. Refinancing and holding achieves this.

This is why refinancing at the end of optimization is the preferred step of most pro real estate investors I know.

The decision to sell or refinance can be made using one fantastic question: *Does this property move me closer or further from my goal?* It's a beautiful (perhaps the most beautiful) question an investor can ask[7].

This question is so simple and elegant, and it peels away all the layers of built-up thought. It brings us back to the very beginning of why we start investing in the first place. If really considered it will take us back to our legacy vision.

The disposition phase can be as strategic as the initial purchase and optimization. To be strategic about this phase, focus on understanding it before you ever make the purchase. Consider the sale when purchasing and optimizing.

Know your exit strategies going in. Clearly understand what a core asset in your niche looks like.

---

[7] Tip of the cap to REIN for this stellar question.

Remain strategic through the process knowing that each step is connected to the others. You never simply acquire a property without considering optimization and disposition, and you never simply optimize that property without letting the process affect your next acquisition and letting it help you consider your next disposition.

How can you make the next move fit the overall direction? How well does this asset synergize with the rest of my portfolio? Would I create more velocity by selling this asset and using the cash to buy a better asset? Or would keeping the property and refinancing it be the best way to move closer to my goal?

Strategy and Emotions

Most real estate books will tell you the only way to succeed is to completely remove emotions from the decision making process. You can't make a proper decision as long as you're acting from emotion, or so the old story goes.

I agree with a caveat. Yes, it's true that no successful investor ever reached the top making purely emotional decisions, but there is a place for emotions in real estate investing.

Don't worry. I'm not going to suggest you abandon reason in favour of emotion. Still, emotions have a place in real estate success so long as you're aware of the emotion at play and are committed to success before emotional fulfillment.

An example of negatively using emotion would be developing a strong aversion to selling a property due to fear of looking foolish. Selling would be proof to your Uncle Joe (or another naysayer) that the building was a dog all along. He warned you not to get involved in real estate after all and told you you'd lose all your money. You don't want to prove old Uncle Joe right, so you determine to keep the property and make it work rather than give Uncle Joe the pleasure of being right.

To effectively use emotions in the disposition phase, we must be aware of the emotion we're seeking to maximize and make sure it's an emotion that will benefit all parties involved.

How does the false pride that might result from proving old Uncle Joe wrong affect everyone involved? Will your spouse feel undue stress in his or her life because you're bleeding cash to hold onto a dog of a property? Do your kids sense you're not present with them because you can't get that dog of a property off your mind? Are you spending weeknights fixing problems because property management can't stay on top of it? Is your accountant concerned that holding this property is unsustainable? These might be signs that proving Uncle Joe wrong isn't worth it. Letting this emotion decide isn't improving anyone's life.

So, what does a positive use of emotion in the disposition phase look like?

First, consider why you became a real estate investor to begin with. Wasn't it to maximize certain emotions and

The Solidifying Strategy

restrict others? We want to feel freedom. We want to feel a sense of self-determination and control over your life. We want to feel a sense of security, which comes with financial security. We want to feel that we're providing for our family or building a positive legacy. This is a positive expression of pride (rather than the false pride about proving Uncle Joe wrong).

Most actions we take are an attempt to maximize certain emotions and to reduce or eliminate others. Real estate can help with this process by treating decisions strategically. The best investors understand the emotions they want to enhance and the path between decisions and results. It's so easy to get caught up in a negative emotion that's counter to our true emotional desire. Greed – for example – destroys more real estate investors than anything else.

I can understand why most real estate professionals suggest removing emotion. It's a simple formula, but I believe it's more powerful to accept and cultivate the emotions we want to enhance and be aware of the role that negative and positive emotions play.

There is nothing wrong with making an emotional decision, so long as you're making that decision with your eyes wide open. When a billionaire buys a sports franchise, they're doing it with house money. They know it's an emotional decision at some level. For them, even a failure of the sports franchise won't bring about their ruin. They're seeking to maximize the emotions around owning a sports team, yet making good decisions below it. It's the best of both worlds.

I'm going to suggest you do the same thing as sports franchise owning billionaires. Do you believe that one of the jobs of a real estate investor is to provide excellent housing to excellent tenants? Does fulfilling this lead you to a feeling of pride? Are you trying to help your team win? If so, then by all means go ahead and buy a building in order to fulfill that emotion, but by all means *do not* do so at the expense of your own success. You're not doing anyone a favour by purchasing a bad building just so you can play out a hero fantasy.

It's only a silly little fantasy if you do so at your own expense or the expense of others. It's not silly if your interests align with helping people. It then becomes a good business decision, which also maximizes the emotion you're after. Yes, you can have it all as a real estate investor. Never settle for less.

CHAPTER 11
Wrapping it All Up

> "The master has failed more times than the beginner has even tried."
>
> Stephan McCranie

Why Strategy is the Difference

We started this book by talking a little bit about my background in the real estate business. I told the story about my early life property management experiences and seeing investors come and go. We're all affected by our life's story. My story is part of what drives me. The entire tone of this book is related to my life's experiences (especially my life's real estate experiences) and the observations based on those experiences.

Without a doubt, seeing the impact my grandparents' portfolio whittled down from 17 down to three multi-family properties over the course of a couple of years was a huge influence on me. This event was a driver of awareness that all is not as it necessarily seems in real estate. Now that he's gone I often miss the opportunity to sit and learn more from him.

The strange thing about real estate is how subcultures inevitably rise up around communities of real estate investors. No doubt this is common in many industries, but it seems especially pronounced in real estate.

In those subcultures there is a high degree of transience. I think this is due to the fact that real estate is often a side business for people with regular jobs. They see real estate as a way out of their restrictive 9 to 5 life.

Well, it sure *can be*, but too many real estate investors are in too much of a rush to get there immediately.

Earlier in this book we discussed Bill, a real life investor whose name and vital details I've changed. I wish I could say Bill's case was a rare one. So many investors come in with *huge* plans and the reality often doesn't match up, hence the transience within the investor subculture.

Seeing these rising stars over the years has only strengthened the belief I developed as I saw my grandparents' portfolio decimated: *staying power is more important than growth.*

In fact, growth becomes natural if staying power is taken care of. Being in a rush without thinking and acting strategically and systematically doesn't work. One must be confident his or her portfolio can last through the worst-case scenarios while at the same time being growth oriented through strategic and systematic action.

In this book, I've laid out a strategic approach that has its entire basis in legacy. Experience has shown me those investors who start with a legacy in mind increase their chances of developing staying power and sustainable growth exponentially.

Those whose only goal is 'getting rich' inevitably flare out and move onto the next thing once they realize the real estate game requires a minimum 10 years hard work before reaching some level of financial autonomy.

There are rare cases of investors that reach financial autonomy before 10 years, but it's these few examples that keep the dream alive in so many others in the subculture. It's a case of the goal being counterproductive.

Better off to think in terms of long-term strategy and develop staying power than try to hit a grand slam right away. Striking out is the most common result of swinging for the fences.

If you really think about it, is 10 years really that long of a wait to develop staying power, huge momentum, long term wealth, and most importantly, legacy?

The Perfect Example

As I was doing research to write this book I met group of investors (Oneka Land Company) that epitomized what I think is the right way to invest in multi-family real estate. In fact, it wouldn't be inappropriate to say that they their example was a template for me in writing many parts of this book.

A single word can summarize their method: strategic. Let's take a look at the steps they took as they built their portfolio:

1. **Legacy Strategy:** Oneka Land Company started with the right vision. They decided from the beginning that they were going to be in the game for the long haul. This meant that they would purchase and maintain excellent properties for the long haul. Their stated goal was to provide excellent.

2. **Niche Strategy:** They were (and still are) laser-beam focused on their tiny niche, which is in the Oliver district of Edmonton. Due to their strict niche focus they have been reaping all of the benefits we've discussed in this book. Their niche-focus is downright impressive. Their focus remains fixed on their niche and they consider only those options that further their growth there or advance strategic goals.

   I've never seen an investor streamline their operations so quickly and seamlessly. Marketing, branding, and management are all smoothly running machines.

3. **Optimization Strategy:** They decided in advance what kind of buildings they were going to buy, where they would buy them, and how they would optimize them. In addition they sought to buy each building in close proximity to each other so they could capitalize on future land and zoning opportunities.

4. **Solidification Strategy:** Oneka Land Company is very much in an active holding phase. To my knowledge they have not sold any of their Edmonton properties, yet. Their initial strategy was to buy and hold in Edmonton through what is promising to be one of the strongest real estate markets in the city's history.

   However, they thought through their plan from the beginning and have taken action to solidify their holdings. Their portfolio is fantastic, which means they are in an excellent position to refinance all of their properties at excellent rates when they need new financing – after their excellent optimization phase.

Oneka Land Company is a very buttoned-down, well-oiled machine. The operators entered the market with years of business acumen and success behind them. This makes them an excellent example to follow.

A Final Note

Strategic success takes time and lots of effort. Nobody learns it all from a single book or even a couple of years of practice. Nobody is perfect, and imperfect action moving forward is superior to doing nothing perfectly. The goal must be to continually improve as a strategic investor. Strategy breeds staying power – and staying power is sexy.

APPENDIX

Metrics for your Real Estate Portfolio

There seem to be three approaches to using data metrics just as in acquisition and management - amateur, professional, and institutional:

1. **Amateur:** The amateur approach is to simply ignore data because it's a scary unknown topic. Whether or not they know it, every real estate investor pays attention to certain data. For example, if you get burned by a certain type of tenant a couple of times, you'll likely shy away from them the next time. This is a rudimentary form of data collection based only on intuition. We can leverage our own (and others') data in far detail than this, though.

2. **Professional:** The professional keeps good records and clearly understands societal and demographic trends. Rather than acting on intuition alone, the professional has plenty of good reasons to take a specific action. They understand how to use the information to make informed decisions, though they often do so inconsistently.

3. **Institutional:** At this level, data collection and analysis is a science. These companies plan years and decades in advance based on their own data collection and the more complicated metrics understood by high-level statisticians. They implement cutting edge technologies to gather and understand the information and make it accessible across their organization.

The point of using data metrics is to make better informed decisions for minimizing certain expenses, maintaining properties more effectively, and increasing income.

Below is a list of 10 metrics that any real estate investor can begin using in his or her path from amateur to professional. Each of these metrics can be simple to measure and help the astute investor to take appropriate action:

1. **Debt to Value (Book and Market)**: At surface level this metric isn't complicated. What's the current market value of your property divided by the current outstanding debt? This metric indicates how much risk you're carrying, your potential ability to refinance, and potential profit if you sell. If depreciating your properties for tax purposes you can also calculate this metric using book value. This will give you a clear picture of your future tax burden or help you convince your investors it's a good idea to pay down more debt now rather than pay a dividend. Remember you can typically depreciate two per cent the first year and four per

cent thereafter. If the building is worth $1 million a two per cent and four per cent yearly depreciation adds up, though it comes back to you as a capital gain when you sell. Knowing how much theoretical equity you have (debt to book value or loan to value) is a good measure of risk. Ensure you know the real numbers for how much you can get out and how much it'll cost you to realize that equity.

2. **Operating Expense Ratio (OER)**: People love this one when they're buying properties. In my opinion (and the actions of bigger companies seem to prove me right) OER is more useful for comparing stabilized buildings, and less accurate a measure in a non-stabilized building. The OER tells us how much we're spending on operational costs, before debt servicing, as a percentage of net income on the building. That's a complex way of saying how much of every dollar of rent is going to pay the bills of the building. This metric will tell you how fast you can get a poor asset under control. REIT's like Mainstreet consider a stabilized building to be one that's been under management for 24 to 36 months.

3. **Occupancy vs. Vacancy**: There are actually two metrics here – first there's vacancy rate. If there's one vacancy in a 20-unit building you have a five per cent vacancy rate in that month, but it's important to know if the suite was empty due to it being unavailable for rent or some other factor. Investors must distinguish vacancy rate as a snapshot metric or a forward-looking estimation.

I prefer to think of the "historical vacancy rate" as the occupancy rate. You come to the occupancy rate by taking the number of total units multiplied by the number of months rented, divided by the number of units divided by the total amount of time. It's usually a trailing average or a running total.

4. **Rent-Days Lost to Renovations** – Renovations take time. As we all know, time is money. How long does it take you to do a renovation?

   If you're doing a similar renovation over and over again, such as new flooring and countertops in every suite, how fast can your crew turn around a suite to be rent-ready?

   While under construction your units are not available for rent, and then when you're done renovations and someone can move in it's now counted as vacant. The most proactive and successful investors I know are almost always able to get into the suite in advance to take care of the small renovations like painting and wall repair.

   To know if your renovation velocity needs improvement you need to track it.

   Every unit comes with 365 rent-days – it's up to you to make sure as many as possible are fully occupied and paid.

   Friendly Caveat: No third-party property manager will track this metric. This is a degree of detail they literally can't manage based on the fees you pay them. The only way to track this metric is by yourself. It's one of several reasons that once you have a reached a critical mass of units you should consider developing your own team to manage some aspects of your property.

The turnover metric is hugely important in in a slow multi-family market. Assuming you can renovate a suite and have it rent-ready the same day your old tenant moves out, which isn't an easy task, we need to ask the question: How long does it take to get a new tenant into the suite?

Same-weekend turnover is the goal and same-day turnover is possible. There are plenty of investors that set and achieve this goal consistently.

The trick is to be in the unit before the tenant moves out in order to do little touchups. Your onsite manager must be able to coordinate moving, carpet cleaning, and touchups. If rent is $1,000 per month every lost day cost $32.88

Go back through your records and record the time lost on every turnover. See if you can minimize turnover time through better organization.

5. **Loss to Lease** – I first saw this metric on a Boardwalk annual report. It measures the difference between the rents collected during the year from tenants on a fixed term lease (e.g. $1,000/month) compared to the full market lease. Imagine a year where full market rent for each month was $950, $975, $975,

$975, $995, $1010, $1050, $1050, $1050, $1050, $1050, $1050. Your leased unit income was $12,000, whereas the market could have been $12,180. Your loss to lease is 1.47 per cent.

To calculate this you will need the market average for you area, which I calculate using www.padmapper.com or something similar. These sites are just aggregators of all the rental information in a given area. From these sites you can find the average lease for a year and will know if you're earning above, on, or below market. If you're below you have a loss to lease. Just a friendly reminder – it's not something you can realistically use on a single unit; you really need to apply it across a building or an area.

6. **Incentives as a Proportion of Rent:** In flat or falling markets, investors will often incentives to tenants so they can fill vacancies.

If you choose to give a discount for the first two months of a lease, or a free TV, or something else like free parking or laundry tokens, then it's vital to measure this. These costs are real and must be tracked.

To measure this, simply apply the cost of the incentive against the rental income.

This metric will give you a clear idea of which suites and buildings require more incentive to keep rented. This information will help you decide which 'dogs' to sell when the next seller's market comes around.

7. **Length of Stay:** This is my favorite metric, because it tells an oft-ignored but incredibly valuable story. Simply, how long have your tenants lived in your property? Knowing this will allow you to begin asking yourself: How can I improve this?

   At a recent REIN meeting, Don Campbell said that area, asset type, and suite mix all affect length of stay. Knowing how long tenants stay in each type will give you a better understanding for making strategic decisions. How much longer do tenants stay in a building with a nice mix of one and two-bedroom suites versus a building made up entirely of one-bedroom suites? Is length of stay related to if you first rented to them with an incentive? Does the free TV bring in tenants who only stay for a year until they can find another owner with a free microwave?

   There is always a cost to turnover. If you have a building where tenants stay multiple years, it means you have a building that doesn't require as much management effort and likely fewer renovations.

   Good data lets you decide what you want to buy moving forward and which assets are underperforming and should be sold.

8. **Maintenance as a Proportion of Expenses** – Like the operating expense ratio item above, you should be keeping track of how much of your expenses are going to repairs and maintenance.

Remember that repairs and maintenance are expenses in your accounting. This is different than capital costs, which you can't claim as expenses.

Believe it or not, this is an expense that *usually too low*, and most investors are slowly running their building into the ground because they're too worried about cash flow. Unfortunately, this is one of those metrics that I can't really provide a rock-solid guideline for. The maintenance will vary depending on many factors.

Total expenses should generally be in the range of 30-40 per cent of gross income. In my market this currently averages out to around $4000 per year. And the maintenance should be at least 15 to 20 percent of the total expenses, which in my market would average out around $600 to $800 per year. Many institutional owners have a minimum amount (often a proportion of the gross income) they'll reinvest into a building ensuring the long-term health of the asset and the protection of their brand.

What really matters is that the building is being properly maintained, and if I see a building with maintenance expenses below 10 per cent of the total expense cost it gives me cause for concern.

9. **Utility Cost per Square Foot:** It's worth measuring total utility costs and calculating how much each square foot is costing you. Utility upgrades are often some of the most cost effective projects in a

Metrics for your Real Estate Portfolio

property. They're many consultants who can help you analyze specific patterns. The simplest measure is just cost per square foot (PSF). You might also consider the cost per person, much the same way a farmer measures pasture per animal unit.

This will help you compare apples to apples, and if you're looking at higher costs in some buildings you should also consider measuring adults or teenagers per unit and maybe square foot per person. The cost of small utility meters for consumption monitoring (but not billing) is making the idea of full-building monitoring a more approachable reality.

Once you decipher the patterns, you will be able to make informed decisions about potentially changing the way you offset the cost of utilities and perhaps building greater efficiencies into your building.

10. **Deferred Capital Costs:** My experience in the multi-family realm along with my experience as treasurer of a condo board has given me a healthy respect for reserve fund studies, which are also known as depreciation reports.

    Simply put, every owner of every multi-family building needs to look at the big expenses and estimate what they cost, their lifespan, and then work backwards to know what you need to save.

    By comparing those coming big expenses against annual revenue or market value you get a clear picture of what the future might hold.

For example, a shingled roof on a house may cost you $5,000 and last 20 years. That means the day after the roof is installed you should save $250 per year for the next new roof.

Does this seem extreme?

Maybe, but I've also seen a huge number of owners, both residential and commercial get screwed when these costs catch up to them.

Just ask the owners at the Oliver Gardens condo building near downtown Edmonton. They were recently put in the difficult position of having to pay a $2.3 million special assessment, which amounts to a $35,000 to $55,000 assessment for each individual unit.

This happened because nobody thought about saving the money to fix issues 20 years ago.

CPSIA information can be obtained
at www.ICGtesting.com
Printed in the USA
BVOW06s2310130917
494857BV00012B/44/P